34: Peking-Washington: Chinese Foreign Policy and the United States

THE WASHINGTON PAPERS
Volume IV

34: Peking-Washington: Chinese Foreign Policy and the United States

Harold C. Hinton

THE CENTER FOR STRATEGIC AND INTERNATIONAL STUDIES
Georgetown University, Washington, D.C.

SAGE PUBLICATIONS
Beverly Hills / London

Printed in the United States of America

For information address:

SAGE PUBLICATIONS, INC.
275 South Beverly Drive
Beverly Hills, California 90212

SAGE PUBLICATIONS LTD
St George's House / 44 Hatton Garden
London EC1N 8ER

ıdard Book Number 0-8039-0649-8

gress Catalog Card No. 76-17373

FIRST PRINTING

*When citing a Washington Paper, please use the proper form. Remember to cite
the series title and include the paper number. One of the two following formats
can be adapted (depending on the style manual used):*

(1) HASSNER, P. (1973) "Europe in the Age of Negotiation." The Washington
Papers, I, 8. Beverly Hills and London: Sage Pubns.

OR

(2) Hassner, Pierre. 1973. *Europe in the Age of Negotiation.* The Washington
Papers, vol. 1, no. 8. Beverly Hills and London: Sage Publications.

CONTENTS

There exist fundamental differences between China and the United States. Owing to the joint efforts of both sides the relations between the two countries have improved to some extent in the last three years, and contacts between the two peoples have developed. The relations between the two countries will continue to improve so long as the principles of the Sino-American Shanghai Communique are carried out in earnest.

Premier Chou En-lai
Report to the Fourth
National People's Congress
January 13, 1975

1. INTRODUCTION: A HISTORIC AFFINITY?

A mericans and Chinese tend to get along well on the person-to-person level; and the chemistry of recent contacts between Chinese and American leaders, as well as between visitors from one of the two countries and residents of the other, has generally been good.

In the case of the Chinese communists, this basic tendency has been reinforced from time to time by the ideological and political sympathy for them felt and expressed by certain Americans, mainly private individuals such as Agnes Smedley and Edgar Snow, rather than by officials.[1] It has also been argued that something like the converse is also true: that the Chinese communist leadership in the mid-1940s wanted a friendly relationship with the United States as a means, at the minimum, of preventing American political and military support for the Chinese Nationalists after the defeat of Japan and of avoiding exclusive dependence on the Soviet Union; and that the failure of such a relationship to materialize was mainly the fault of American policy.[2] The author has heard a distinguished Soviet China specialist maintain that there has been a kind of historic affinity between the United States and the Chinese communist movement—the latter being, in his judgment, not truly Marxist-Leninist—and that the only prohibitive obstacle to friendly relations since 1950 has been the American commitment to Taiwan.

By its nature, this line of argument cannot be fully proved or disproved. It clearly has some truth in it. American support for, and above all American military aid to, the Chinese Nationalists in connection with their war effort against the communists after V-J Day certainly destroyed any real possibility of friendly relations at that time between the communists and the United States. Whether this was a mistake on the part of the United States, and what would have happened had there been no such aid and support, is another matter. In any case, the communists won their civil war, and it might be supposed that there then existed a chance for a fresh start in their relationship with the United States but that this chance was ruined by the Korean War, American protection of Taiwan, and the close relationship between the United States and Japan, which taken as a whole suggested to Peking a possible American intention to try to overthrow the new communist regime in China and not merely to deny it control over Taiwan.

This line of argument, plausible though it is, represents a serious oversimplification, because it ignores the Chinese communist movement's close historic contact with Soviet communism and its remarkable love-hate relationship with Stalin, although this too is a point that can be overstressed. The outbreak of the Soviet-American Cold War coincided roughly with the adoption of the American policy of support for the Nationalists in the Chinese civil war, and there was no way in which an important communist party like the Chinese could remain uncommitted with respect to the Cold War, even if it wished to do so, without incurring Stalin's open and dangerous displeasure. The Chinese communists similarly had to commit themselves when the Stalin-Tito controversy erupted in 1948, and their unavoidable choice in favor of Stalin tended to determine their support for him against Truman as well as against Tito. This decision was made clear in an important tract published by Liu Shao-ch'i (1951), then the second-ranking figure in the party, in November 1948. In this document—written more than six months before Mao Tse-tung's better-known declaration (1967: 302-315, esp. 306) that the

Chinese communists "leaned" toward the Soviet side and away from the United States and almost two years before the outbreak of the Korean War—Liu clearly signaled the choice indicated. There is no reason to believe that the choice was reconsidered, and there is abundant evidence of a doctrinaire pro-Sovietism and anti-Americanism on the part of the Chinese communists during the early 1950s.[3]

The historical record, then, points fairly clearly toward the conclusion that there is no significant historic affinity, at the official level at any rate, between the Chinese communists and the United States. The current Sino-American détente exists, as far as the Chinese side is concerned, not because they love the United States, but because they need it. This need is real, but it is not total, and it is not necessarily permanent. How and why the détente arose, and what its future might be, are the main subjects of this study.

2. THE "HATE AMERICA" PHASE

Today it requires something of an intellectual effort to recall the era when the relationship between the United States and the Chinese Communist Party was one of intense and articulate hostility. The effort is worth making, both because it suggests the seriousness of the forces that must have been required to generate a détente between the two adversaries and because it reminds us that what happened once could happen again.

The United States and the Chinese Civil War

As the end of the war against Japan approached, Mao Tse-tung thought fit, for reasons already suggested, to profess a favorable attitude toward the United States. For example, in his important report "On Coalition Government," delivered to the Chinese Communist Party's Seventh Congress in April 1945, he praised the United States for its role in the Pacific war and its impending liberation of the Philippines from colonial status (Mao Tse-tung hsuan chi, 1948: 287-352).[4]

Probably the most important American to reciprocate this friendly feeling, more or less, had been General Joseph W. Stilwell, who had favored making Lend-Lease equipment available to the Chinese communist forces in order to improve their performance against the Japanese (Tuchman, 1971: 485).

After General Stilwell's relief from command in October 1944, however, the U.S. government was clearly committed as it had been before to the support of the National government under Chiang Kai-shek against its enemies foreign and domestic. As early as August 10, 1945, accordingly, General Stilwell's successor, General Albert C. Wedemeyer, was directed by the Joint Chiefs of Staff to provide transport and logistical support to Chinese Nationalist forces seeking to occupy territory currently held by the Imperial Japanese Army, which was about to surrender; General Wedemeyer was ordered, however, not to involve American ground forces in combat, presumably meaning combat with the Chinese communists (U.S. Government, 1969: 527-528). This directive led to large-scale American cooperation in the movement of Chinese Nationalist forces into the lower Yangtze Valley, North China, and Manchuria, much to the detriment of the simultaneous effort by the communists to occupy as much as possible of the territory being evacuated by the Japanese.

This American effort, which was accompanied by the presence of some American combat units in the coastal region of North China, angered the communists and evoked loud protests from them to the effect that the United States was intervening in the Chinese civil war (Chou En-lai, 1949: 706-710). Communist resentment on this score undoubtedly made an important, although by no means the decisive, contribution to the ultimate failure of the complex American effort, under the auspices of Ambassador Patrick J. Hurley and then of General George C. Marshall, to mediate the conflict between the Nationalists and the communists (Tang Tsou, 1963: ch. VIII-X). By the beginning of 1947, after General Marshall's departure from China, Chinese communist propagandists were attacking the United States not only for its role in China but on a more generalized ideological basis, as the leader of the "imperialist camp" since the end of the Second World War (Lu Ting-yi, 1949: 710-719).

"We Lean to One Side"

As already indicated, the Stalin-Tito controversy of 1948 led the Chinese Communist Party to side with the leader of the "socialist camp" not only against the Yugoslav dissenter but, more clearly than before, against the United States as well. The official Chinese communist mood at that time was both strongly pro-Soviet and militantly anti-American (see Mao Tse-tung, 1967: 302-315; 1961: vol. 4, 172; also U.S. Government, 1975: vol. VIII). It is quite likely that the communist leadership, reasoning by analogy with the history of Allied intervention against the Bolsheviks after 1917, feared some sort of American action against itself; this fear became especially acute for a time after the beginning of American involvement in the Korean War, Korea having been a spring-board in earlier times for Japanese military moves against Manchuria and North China.

For this reason as well as others, the Chinese Communist Party "leaned to one side" and sought a patron, ally, and ideological leader in Stalin's Russia. The Sino-Soviet alliance concluded on February 14, 1950, was directed against Japan or "any other State which should unite with Japan, directly or indirectly, in acts of aggression" meaning the United States (text of treaty in Beloff, 1953: 260-262). It was supplemented by a program of Soviet economic and military aid to the People's Republic of China and by a generally close political relationship between the two allies (see Hinton, 1974: 124-125). Probably the most important action taken by this combination during the remainder of Stalin's lifetime was the launching, in close coordination of course with Kim Il Song's regime, of the Korean War in June 1950.

By the outbreak of the war, the Chinese Communist Party's "lean-to-one-side" policy, and above all its action in allying itself formally with the U.S.'s adversary in the Cold War, had turned the U.S. government against Peking and spoiled the already slight chances for a serious American attempt at a rapprochement between them (Acheson, 1951: 792).[5]

Ambitions for Revolutionary Leadership in Asia

During their discussions in Moscow (December 1949-February 1950), Stalin and Mao appear to have agreed that communist strategy for Northeast Asia, the area where the United States was most strongly committed, should be determined largely by the Soviet Union. The region where a corresponding role seems to have been claimed by and conceded to Peking, Southeast and perhaps South Asia, was not one of special concern to the United States at that time. Yet an appearance, and still more the reality, of Chinese expansionist tendencies of any kind toward the south would be bound to create antagonism between Peking and the United States. This antagonism, the need for and extent of which was exaggerated in the thinking and propaganda of both sides, emerged during the 1950s and had a great deal to do with the formulation of the American containment-and-isolation policy toward the People's Republic of China (PRC).

By 1949, the Chinese communists had formed a highly self-satisfied image of the validity and significance of their own revolutionary experience, of which "armed struggle" (organized warfare, guerrilla and/or regular) was a central feature, for other Asian peoples. This idea was loudly set forth for the consideration of Asian peoples in the Chinese communists' message of greeting to the so-called Calcutta Youth Conference in February 1948 (North Shensi radio, 1948), and in Liu Shao-ch'i's better known speech to the Peking meeting of the communist-controlled World Federation of Trade Unions in November 1949.[6] In mid-1951, Peking went so far as to deny that the Soviet revolutionary model, and by implication Soviet leadership, had any relevance to the developing countries (Lu Ting-yi, 1951). This was apparently too much for Moscow, and the effect of the Chinese claim was weakened, to say the least, by heavy defeats suffered in Korea in April and May 1951. A few months later, an authoritative Soviet spokesman denied that the Chinese Communist Party's revolutionary experience constituted a "stereotype" for the rest of Asia (Hinton, 1966: 70).

The Chinese Communist Party emphatically spoke, and presumably also thought, of its moral, political, and limited material support for communist revolutionary movements in southern Asia after 1948 as essentially anti-"imperialist" in purpose, and it considered the United States to be the leader of the "imperialist camp." Conversely, the United States tended officially to view the PRC as, among other things, essentially a Soviet agent trying to promote the communization of Asia.[7]

The Korean War

Nothing else did so much to create Sino-American hostility as the Korean conflict, for the obvious reason that it involved an undeclared war between American forces and Chinese "volunteers."[8] The war launched the real beginning of the "Hate America" phase of Chinese foreign policy. The American intervention in the Korean War, and above all General MacArthur's insistence on driving to the Manchurian border, seemed to Peking to pose a serious threat to its security, and yet at the same time seemed a magnificent issue over which to seek increased support from the Chinese public and the international left, including the Soviet Union.[9]

From Peking's point of view, the Korean War produced a political challenge almost as serious as the military one. This was the decision of 70 percent of the 20,000 Chinese prisoners taken in Korea to refuse repatriation. This refusal, which Peking took to be the result of American and Chinese Nationalist coercion or trickery, amounted to a rejection of the new Chinese regime's legitimacy by men of whom it felt it had the greatest possible right to expect loyalty. Peking's initial reaction was to refuse to sign an armistice that would permit voluntary, as opposed to compulsory, repatriation. It persisted in this stand until early 1953, when the newly inaugurated Eisenhower administration threatened it with nuclear weapons unless it signed an armistice and the death of Stalin deprived it of the hope of active Soviet support. After a few months of further bargaining, Peking signed an armistice agreement on July 27, 1953, that did in fact incorporate the principle of voluntary repatriation (Hinton, 1966: ch. 8).

From this painful experience, which cost the PRC several hundred thousand military casualties, Peking evidently derived a firm conviction that it did not want to fight another war with the United States anywhere, and that it did not favor any sort of destabilization of the Korean peninsula because of the riskiness of such a development in so strategically sensitive an area.

The First Indochina War and SEATO

Apart from Korea, the main area of Peking's involvement in hostilities outside its borders in the early years was Vietnam. Peking felt a greater sense of political sympathy for and commitment to Ho Chi Minh's regime than to Kim Il Song's, which was essentially a Soviet satellite down to the Korean War. On the other hand, the fact that the Viet Minh was never threatened with defeat by the French and regarded China as the traditional enemy, and that Peking was preoccupied with Korea until mid-1953, called for a more limited Chinese involvement than in the case of Korea.

As the Korean War wound down, however, Peking stepped up its military aid to the Viet Minh and made a decisive material contribution to the successful siege of Dienbienphu in the spring of 1954. Although there was no need for Peking to intervene directly in Vietnam, Secretary Dulles chose to allege that such an intervention was probable, and that if it occurred the PRC would be the target of some sort of massive retaliation. His real purpose was apparently to create an atmosphere of crisis conducive to the formation of the Southeast Asia Treaty Organization (SEATO), which he intended both as a barrier to Chinese expansion in the region and as a diplomatic monument to himself.

At the ensuing Geneva Conference, Peking still felt sufficiently threatened by the United States that it made critical diplomatic concessions at the expense of its Vietnamese allies. On the other hand, it insisted for its own protection that the United States be prohibited from maintaining military bases or forces in Indochina and that the United States sign the final agreement emerging from the conference. The United States refused to sign this agreement, mainly because Dulles did not want to cosign an agreement with the PRC that appeared to "lose" some territory to the communist adversary, although the United States did promise not to "disturb" the agreement by force. Peking had to be content with this, and with the fact that, if observed, the agreement would rule out American bases and forces in Indochina.

Given its profound distrust of the United States and of Dulles in particular, Peking regarded SEATO not merely as a defensive but as an aggressive anticommunist and anti-Chinese organization. SEATO was not much more popular with the neutral governments of South and Southeast Asia, and perhaps the main immediate result of SEATO's formation was a closer relationship between these neutral countries and Peking that began to become an important feature of Asian international politics about the time of the Bandung Conference of April 1955. In addition, SEATO remained an irritant in Sino-American relations and a target of Chinese propaganda attacks (Hinton, 1966: ch. 9; Gurtov, 1967).[10]

The American "Occupation" of Taiwan

The extension of American protection to Taiwan on June 27, 1950, promptly became an issue in Sino-American relations second in importance only to the Korean War, and one of longer duration. Peking began to refer to the American initiative as an occupation of Taiwan, an obviously exaggerated position that flowed not merely from resentment of American intervention in the continuing Chinese civil war but from a more specific consideration. Since Taiwan was regarded in both Peking and Taipei as Chinese territory, even an alleged American occupation of it gave Peking a basis for invoking active Soviet support under the terms of the Sino-Soviet alliance. For at least as long as the Korean War and the Indochina crisis lasted, however, there was no real opportunity for either Peking or Moscow to take action on Taiwan. The Eisenhower administration's action of February 1953 in "unleashing" Chiang Kai-shek produced no effect on the mainland, since the Nationalists had no significant offensive capability and the United States was obviously doing little more than trying to frighten Peking into agreeing to an armistice in Korea.

As soon as the Geneva Conference was over, Peking gave signs of believing that the time had come to try making progress on the Taiwan question. A propaganda campaign announcing an imminent "liberation" of the island escalated in September 1954 to a six-month series of intermittent shellings of the Nationalist-held offshore island of Quemoy and air and sea clashes in the Taiwan Strait. The Soviet Union showed no interest in supporting its Chinese allies, even during an important visit that Khrushchev paid to Peking shortly after the beginning of the crisis, and even after the United States signed a mutual security agreement (in effect, an alliance) with the Republic of China at the end of the year, while Congress in the so-called Formosa Resolution gave the president conditional authority to defend the offshore islands against a communist attack, provided it appeared to be part of an attack on Taiwan itself. To Peking the institutionalization in treaty form of the security relationship between Washington and Taipei was a very serious development. The fact that Moscow showed no inclination to take any effective counteraction, such as threatening West Berlin, seems to have contributed significantly to the origins of the Sino-Soviet dispute, even though little was said about this aspect of it in public on either side.

Given the absence of significant Soviet support, Peking saw no alternative to trying to promote international backing for its position and international pressure on the United States by portraying itself as the innocent and injured party in the dispute over Taiwan. This it did with considerable effect at the Bandung Conference, where Premier Chou En-lai announced Peking's willingness to negotiate the status of Taiwan with the United States. This it actually did at a series of conversations at the ambassadorial level with the United States at Geneva, beginning in August 1955. There was no progress, however, since the positions of the two sides were incompatible. The American side demanded a "renunciation of force" by Peking with respect to Taiwan, something that Peking was unwilling on principle to concede since it regarded its conflict with the Nationalists as exclusively a civil war. Peking's position was that the United

States should terminate its military protection, or "occupation," of Taiwan.

In view of the lack of progress at Geneva, Peking began early in 1956 to encourage feeling in favor of an accommodation on the part of the Nationalist leadership, but without any significant effect. It also tried to influence official and public opinion in the United States by claiming to favor the initiation of Sino-American trade and an exchange of correspondents, but with no concrete results.

From late August to early October 1958, Peking initiated a serious military crisis in the Taiwan Strait designed to parallel the Great Leap Forward at home, to produce a split between the Nationalists and the United States, to smoke out the Soviet attitude, and if possible to promote the "liberation" of Taiwan as well as the offshore islands. Khrushshev provided no useful support apart from rhetoric, and the Nationalists received effective military and political cooperation from the United States to cope with the crisis, from which Peking accordingly emerged one down rather than one up. To console itself, it published in late October 1958 the famous collection of anti-American statements by Mao Tse-tung entitled: *Imperialists and All Reactionaries Are Paper Tigers.* The main, although implicit, theme of this tract seems to be that the United States, although a political "paper tiger," is militarily too strong and dangerous to be confronted directly, even in a situation as carefully controlled as the just-concluded Taiwan Strait crisis; instead, the task of doing in American "imperialism" was to be performed, it was hoped, by the "revolutionary people of the world."

Peking continued to fear that the United States might support an attack on the mainland by the Nationalists, whose armed forces were considerably strengthened by American aid following the Taiwan Strait crisis. In the spring of 1962, when the mainland was barely beginning to recover from the serious economic setback inflicted by the Great Leap Forward, the Nationalists appeared to be planning an attack on the mainland. As a deterrent, Peking heavily reinforced its troops opposite Taiwan. It also sought to smoke out the American attitude by loudly accusing the United States of intending to support a Nationalist "return to the mainland." This drew a denial from the United States at Warsaw, where the Sino-American ambassadorial talks had been held since September 1958, and from President Kennedy himself in a seemingly authoritative remark made at a press conference on June 27, 1962.

Although encouraging as far as it went, this outcome left the American defensive commitment to Taiwan intact. Without its termination, there was little chance of the island's "liberation" by Peking (Young, 1968: ch. 4, 6-8, 10; Hinton, 1966: ch. 10).

The American Containment-and-Isolation Policy

After the outbreak of the Korean War, the United States proceeded to create a powerful security posture in the Far East and the Western Pacific that was designed primarily to contain the PRC and deter its supposed expansionist tendencies. This posture consisted of a network of American military bases, especially those on Okinawa, bilateral and multilateral alliances with friendly or threatened states, and economic and military aid programs.

Along with this went an American effort, less successful and less formidable but still effective to some extent, to isolate the PRC from normal external contacts, including representation in the United Nations, diplomatic recognition, and trade. The United States, of course, maintained a total embargo in all these fields, except for the ambassadorial talks, and encouraged others to do the same. In practice, however, it had to tolerate the fact that many countries, not only communists and neutrals but even allies of the United States, recognized the PRC and traded with it in nonstrategic, and sometimes even strategic, commodities (Hinton, 1975a: 51-56).

Since Peking did not contemplate anything that it regarded as expansion, as distinct from support for leftist revolutionary movements, it believed that the American containment-and-isolation policy was not genuinely defensive or deterrent but was aggressive in purpose. Peking tried to cope with this perceived threat by all the means at its disposal: gradual modernization of its armed forces, including the creation of a nuclear capability after 1957 with substantial Soviet aid; the cultivation of the Sino-Soviet alliance, for whatever it might be worth; tactical caution in crisis situations; and the promotion through propaganda and diplomacy of the highest possible level of pro-Chinese and anti-American feeling abroad.

Peking's Bandung Phase

Beginning about 1952, Peking, like Moscow, greatly reduced its subversive efforts and hostile propaganda against the non-communist governments of Asia and proceeded gradually to woo some of them, India in particular. There were several reasons for this important shift, including the fact that earlier communist revolutionary efforts in the region had not done well, except of course in Vietnam. But the most important reason was probably that Peking felt the need for diplomatic and moral support from as many Asian governments as possible, and from India's above all, in the face of the perceived threat from the United States, which after 1954 was symbolized by and institutionalized in SEATO. Probably the high point of Peking's wooing of the noncommunist, and especially the nonaligned, nations of Asia was the Bandung (or Asian-African) Conference of April 1955, where Chou En-lai made a very favorable impression on his own behalf and that of his government.

A common anti-Americanism, of greatly varying intensity, proved an insufficient bond to preserve an effective community of interest among Peking and its Bandung friends. If India was the most important of the latter, it was also, unfortunately for Peking, the one with which the PRC had the most serious conflicts of interest: rivalry for leadership in Asia, differences over Tibet, and a boundary dispute. By about the beginning of 1957, these issues had begun to come to the surface, and after the middle of the year, for other reasons as well, Peking once more placed its main hopes for progress in its struggle with American "imperialism" on the Soviet Union rather than on the Asian neutrals (Hinton, 1975a: 63-67).

The Sino-Soviet Dispute

Probably the most serious single issue in the Sino-Soviet dispute, which began in the mid-1950s, was over strategy and policy toward the United States; the differences relating to Taiwan have already been discussed. To Peking, the proceedings of the Soviet Twentieth Party Congress (February 1956) suggested a deplorable reluctance on Khrushchev's part to confront American "imperialism" on behalf of China, communist revolutions elsewhere, or even the Soviet Union itself. After the Hungarian crisis of November 1956, Peking gave loud support to Soviet "leadership" over the other communist states, China included, with the clear implication that leadership connoted Soviet responsibility to promote their interests, including those of Peking as against the United States. Khrushchev appeared to be grateful for Chinese support, but there was no indication of a strong Soviet line in dealing with the United States.

The situation appeared to improve somewhat after mid-1957, from Peking's point of view. Khrushchev purged some of his colleagues who evidently favored a more cautious foreign policy: Malenkov and Molotov in June and Marshal Zhukov in October. Soviet successes in space, and especially the orbiting of the first earth satellite (Sputnik I) on October 4, had a tremendous psychological impact on the world, including the United States. Mao Tse-tung, who was looking for a way to recover from the political wounds inflicted by the failure of his Hundred Flowers campaign for free public discussion, thought he had found it in the direction of Moscow. In November 1957 he began to urge a more active anti-American strategy on Khrushchev, under the slogan, "The East wind has prevailed over the West wind." Khrushchev was reluctant to comply, except to some extent in appearance, but he made an important and unique commitment in October-November 1957 in the form of a secret agreement to help the PRC develop nuclear weapons and surface-to-surface missiles. Mao was not satisfied, and his next move, made in the spring of 1958, was to launch a loud propaganda offensive against Tito, one of whose failings in Chinese eyes was his opposition to the strong anti-American line advocated by Peking.

What Mao regarded as Khrushchev's irresolution during the Middle Eastern crisis of 1958 and his lack of enthusiasm for Mao's politico-military offensive in the Taiwan Strait in the same year virtually completed the process of convincing Mao that Khrushchev had no intention of taking a strong anti-American stand, except perhaps over Berlin. In fact, after the death of Secretary Dulles in April 1959, Khrushchev swung to a policy of détente with the United States. In June he cancelled his nuclear aid agreement with the PRC, and in September he indicated cautious support for the Indian side in the escalating Sino-Indian border dispute. When he visited Peking at the end of September, his reception was a chilly one.

In the spring of 1960, Peking launched a furious propaganda attack on Khrushchev, although without referring to him by name, for his insufficient willingness to confront the United States. Khrushchev responded in kind, and the issues were inconclusively debated at a major international conference of communist parties held at Moscow in November-December 1960.[11]

It seems likely that some of Khrushchev's colleagues were less anti-Chinese than he, and that one of the reasons for his attempt to introduce offensive missiles into Cuba in 1962 was to gain leverage on the United States with which to compel it to abandon its protection of Taiwan and in this way promote a major improvement in Sino-Soviet relations. When he decided under a virtual American ultimatum to withdraw the missiles, Peking was furious. The final blow was Khrushchev's signature of the limited nuclear test ban agreement in July 1963, which Peking took to be the ultimate to date in his betrayal of the "socialist camp" for the sake of "colluding" with the "imperialist camp." Sino-Soviet relations were extremely tense from then to Khrushchev's fall from power in October 1964.[12]

Since 1959 or 1960, Peking had in effect been following a policy of waging simultaneous political struggles, with some military overtones, although it was hoped short of war, against American "imperialism" and Soviet "revisionism." This policy is sometimes referred to as the dual adversary strategy. In reality, Peking's obsession with the Sino-Soviet dispute was so intense that it unadmittedly relegated the anti-American struggle to second place, even though as we have seen one of the main original causes of the outbreak of the Sino-Soviet dispute had been Peking's anti-American militancy and its belief that the Soviet Union was not doing enough in the fight against "imperialism."

Escalation in Vietnam

The fall of Ngo Dinh Diem in November 1963 set in motion a process of escalation. Intensifying North Vietnamese and Viet Cong pressures on South Vietnam were answered by growing American involvement culminating in the commitment of American combat forces after February 1965. Among the predictable results was a great upsurge of anti-American feeling in the PRC. At the same time, in accordance with the rationale of the dual adversary strategy, Peking rejected an offer by Khrushchev's successors of an accommodation that would have included co-operation ("united action") on Vietnam.

After a period of debate within the leadership, Peking settled in late 1965 on a strategy for Vietnam that involved loud propaganda support for Hanoi and the Viet Cong but only limited material support (mainly logistical), encouragement of them to fight a "protracted war" and avoid both risky acts of escalation and negotiations with the adversary, propaganda attacks on the United States combined with an absence of actual provocation, intensification of efforts to promote "anti-imperialist" revolutions elsewhere in the Third World, and continued rejection of any sort of cooperation with the Soviet Union apart from trans-shipment of some Soviet equipment across China by rail to North Vietnam. This was the approach favored by Defense Minister Lin Piao (1965), and apparently by Mao himself. Similarly, Peking was distressed by Hanoi's decision in April 1968 to begin negotiations with the United States, although Chinese objections were not allowed to become so articulate as to produce an open controversy with the North Vietnamese (Hinton, 1968: 201-224).

The Cultural Revolution

In many ways the Cultural Revolution (1966-1968) was more an anti-Soviet than an anti-American phenomenon, to the extent that it had an external aspect. Massive anti-Soviet demonstrations in Peking and along the Sino-Soviet border, for example, contrasted conspicuously with an absence of violence against American personnel and facilities in Hong Kong. This was partly because the Cultural Revolution was essentially a domestic Chinese ideological and political movement, to whose concerns Soviet "revisionism" appeared relevant—in a negative sense, of course—in a way that American "imperialism" did not. Furthermore, the United States was demonstrating in Vietnam that it was genuinely dangerous if excessively provoked, whereas the Soviet Union had given no such demonstration since 1956.

The United States nevertheless continued during the Cultural Revolution to be a prime target of Chinese propaganda attacks, in particular for its role in Vietnam. The activities of the American academic left were hailed in the Chinese press as portending some major social revolution (Yuan-li Wu, 1969).

3. FORERUNNERS OF CHANGE

Beneath the surface of continuing Sino-American hostility, some forces for change were at work by the mid-1960s, although more on the American side than on the Chinese.

The Shifting American Attitude

By that time, the fact that the Sino-Soviet relationship was one of contention rather than "monolithic" solidarity had fairly thoroughly penetrated the American official and public consciousness. This was more important, in the long run, than the fact that Peking then appeared to be the more militantly anti-American of the two communist adversaries. In this way the foundations were laid for a future American policy of discriminating significantly between them.

The mere passage of more than a decade since the end of the Korean War, without the occurrence of anything similar, had tended to dull public hostility in the United States toward the PRC, since hostility was not artificially kept alive by official propaganda as it was in China—or at least not to the same degree. In fact, a substantial number of influential Americans in various fields favored with increasing articulateness a policy of seeking actively to establish contacts with the PRC and of "bringing it into the world community," including the United Nations, in order to modify its attitudes and policies in directions more conducive to peace and international stability. The American business community felt a considerable interest in trying to persuade both Peking and Washington to agree to the initiation of Sino-American trade in nonstrategic commodities, the PRC being then the largest inaccessible market in the world (Dulles, 1972).

Tacit Understanding on Vietnam

Both Peking and Washington feared for a time that the Vietnam war might bring on another Sino-American conflict like the one in Korea, and both were eager to avoid such an eventuality. It appears that at Warsaw, in mid-March 1966, the two sides reached what amounted to a tacit understanding: As long as the United States did not attack the PRC, the latter would not intervene in Vietnam, and vice versa (New York Times, 1967). About that time American official and public opinion, fearful that the United States and the PRC might be on a "collision course" over Vietnam, became more outspoken in favoring a policy of "containment without isolation," or what President Johnson called reconciliation with the PRC. [13] At the same time, Moscow began to give signs of believing that the PRC and the United States were on a "collusion course" that was directed against the Soviet Union and could be seriously disadvantageous to Soviet interests.[14]

Except for a brief flurry of alarm when the United States began to base B-52s in Thailand in February 1967, Peking became fairly confident that the United States would not attack China on account of the conflict in Vietnam, or for any other reason, as long as the PRC did not resort to force against an American ally. The perception of the United States as not merely an adversary but a threat and a bully began to fade. Before this happened, nothing but a fundamental adversary relationship was possible. But as the perception in Peking started to change, more or less parallel to the changing perception in the United States, new possibilities began to emerge.

The End of the Cultural Revolution

Another change that had to take place before a significant improvement in Sino-American relations could occur was the end of the Cultural Revolution, which for more than two years froze Chinese foreign policy in a sterile posture of ideological militancy and hostility to nearly everyone. This happened in late 1968, for reasons unconnected with the United States, when the Red Guards, the symbols and cutting edge of the Cultural Revolution, were suppressed by the army at Mao Tse-tung's reluctant command.

In mid-May 1969, only a fortnight after the Chinese Ninth Party Congress had implicitly signaled the termination of the Cultural Revolution, Peking began to send ambassadors to those countries with which it had diplomatic relations, all of its ambassadors but one having been withdrawn early in the Cultural Revolution. A parallel search for diplomatic recognition by governments willing to break with the Republic of China achieved an important initial success with Canada in October 1970, and others followed in rapid succession including Japan and West Germany. A major landmark in Peking's rapid recovery from the effect of the Cultural Revolution on its foreign relations and in its campaign to strengthen its diplomatic position was its admission to the United Nations in October 1971 with the support of the United States, although the United States of course unsuccessfully opposed the expulsion of the Republic of China, which Peking insisted was the indispensable precondition for its own entry (Hinton, 1973a: 283-287).

The Erosion of American Containment

To some although by no means all American officials, the Vietnam conflict was the major means by which the United States was deterring or containing the supposed expansionist tendencies of the PRC. Accordingly, when the United States decided to "wind down" the war in Vietnam in order to move toward an ultimate withdrawal, as it did in effect at the time of President Johnson's celebrated speech of March 31, 1968, the heart more or less went out of the determination to continue containment, as distinct from a more passive deterrence, of the PRC.

The Nixon Doctrine, announced with considerable fanfare in July 1969, stated that the United States would provide a "shield" against a possible threat by a nuclear power—meaning typically the PRC, the wording being unclear as to whether only a nuclear threat or a conventional threat as well was covered—against any state that was allied with the United States or whose security was considered important by the United States to American security or to that of the region. In effect, the doctrine signaled an intent to withdraw from Indochina and reduce American force levels throughout the Far East and the Western Pacific, for domestic reasons for the most part, while retaining it was hoped an active and influential military presence and political role in the region. The implicit reference to the PRC was more a warning to Peking not to take advantage of American disengagement than an indication of a serious expectation that the PRC might try to do so.[15]

The Sino-Soviet Confrontation

The ending of the intensely anti-"revisionist" Cultural Revolution might have been expected to produce an improvement in Sino-Soviet relations. The opposite happened, however, for two main reasons. In the first place, the Soviet Union invaded Czechoslovakia; the reasons were unconnected with China, but the invasion produced serious apprehension in Peking that China might be the next target of Moscow's machismo. Secondly, Defense Minister Lin Piao, the most primitive Maoist and most anti-Soviet of the top Chinese leaders, had emerged from the Cultural Revolution as Mao's heir apparent.

Lin evidently decided that, in the words of a Maoist saying, when confronted with a wild beast one ought not to show the slightest fear. More precisely, he hoped both to deter the Soviet "revisionists" and create an atmosphere of confrontation that he considered suitable for his forthcoming proclamation as Mao's heir at the Ninth Party Congress by staging a clash on the Sino-Soviet border. He probably calculated that a crisis over West Berlin in which Moscow became involved in February 1969 would help to prevent Soviet retaliation against the PRC on any serious level.

Following two armed clashes on the Ussuri River (March 2 and 15, 1969) between Chinese and Soviet troops, the first of which appears to have been initiated by the Chinese side and the second by the Soviet, a major crisis developed. Moscow rapidly strengthened its forces near the Chinese border, demanded that Peking agree to talks on the border issue, and strongly implied that war was the alternative. Under this extreme pressure Peking yielded, although apparently with reluctance on the part of the radical (or Maoist) section of the leadership, and prolonged and inconclusive border talks began on October 20, 1969. In spite of the talks, the threatening Soviet presence to the north remained the dominant factor in Peking's foreign policy calculations (Hinton, 1971).

Warsaw: To Meet or Not to Meet?

Peking, while still in the throes of the Cultural Revolution, had cancelled the Warsaw ambassadorial talks with the United States in the spring of 1968 on the ground that there was "nothing to discuss." But on November 25, 1968, Peking invited the United States, or to be more exact the incoming Nixon administration, to resume the talks on February 20, 1969. This reversal was rationalized by the simultaneous publication of a 1949 statement by Mao in which he indicated that there are times when it is legitimate and even necessary to negotiate with the adversary. The Chinese publicity on the invitation repeated Peking's demand that the United States withdraw its military protection from Taiwan and proposed that the PRC and the United States "conclude an agreement on the Five Principles of Peaceful Coexistence," propositions presumably calculated to appeal to the Chinese radicals.

The appeal was not great enough. By the end of the year, it appeared that somebody, perhaps Lin Piao, had convinced Mao that the dual adversary strategy should remain in full force in spite of the seeming threat from the Soviet Union. Chinese propaganda began to attack the Nixon administration shortly after its inauguration. On the eve of the scheduled talks at Warsaw, Peking cancelled them, allegedly out of anger at the defection to the United States a fortnight earlier of a Chinese diplomat stationed in the Netherlands. Peking gave no sign of interest in resuming the talks at some future date.

The talks were in fact resumed, on January 20 and February 20, 1970; by that time the United States was eager for Chinese help in working out a Vietnam settlement, and Peking was under Soviet pressure to a much greater extent than it had been a year earlier. At the second of these meetings, Peking indicated a willingness to receive a high level American delegation (Hinton, 1971: 32-35, 45).

4. PEKING'S APPROACH TO DÉTENTE

The idea of a détente with the American "imperialist" adversary of two decades standing represented a major shift in Chinese foreign policy, and one basically unacceptable to important radical elements of the leadership. The détente obviously required a convincing rationale, one that would at least quiet if not eliminate the reservations felt by its opponents.

Peking's Motives: The Soviet Union, Taiwan, Technology

To the radicals, and to puzzled officials down the line, the Mao Tse-tung/Chou En-lai mainstream of the Chinese leadership maintained that the opening to the United States, and the contemplated invitation to President Nixon in particular, represented a great triumph for Mao's "revolutionary diplomatic line." According to this explanation, Nixon had admitted the failure of the American policy of containing the PRC by relaxing restrictions on trade and travel, by expressing an interest in visiting the PRC, and above all by beginning to withdraw from Vietnam. Under these circumstances, it was alleged, the opening to the United States would throw the Soviet Union off balance, aggravate the "contradictions" between the United States on the one hand and its Asian "lackeys" and the Soviet Union on the other, and promote the "liberation" of Taiwan in the long run (Institute of International Relations, 1974: 15-17).

There was some validity in this argument. As the following section indicates, the United States had to meet certain conditions in Chinese eyes before Peking, eager though its prevailing elements were for a better relationship with the United States, would agree to take steps in that direction. The real Chinese purpose, however, corresponded more closely with what Peking regarded as the probable results of the new relationship.

Peking's prime concern in its opening to the United States has been to reduce the likelihood of a Soviet attack on the PRC, or so the official argument just paraphrased suggests, and as most foreign observers have come to agree. At the minimum, Peking wanted to feel free of an American threat, whether on account of the Vietnam war or something else, in order to be able to concentrate its energies on dealing with the Soviet threat. An alliance with or a nuclear guarantee by the United States has apparently never been seriously considered on either side, because it would constitute too drastic a departure from current policy; it would also be regarded in the Soviet Union as highly provocative. The role that Peking has wished the United States to play in helping to restrain Soviet violence against China could perhaps be best described as that of a counterweight, a significant negative factor of uncertain proportions in the decision-making process in Moscow. Peking has of course not relied exclusively on the United States to restrain the Soviet Union; it has also improved its own military readiness, conventional as well as nuclear, and cultivated a broad range of potentially useful diplomatic relationships in addition to its opening to the United States. This spectrum of constraints, plus such considerations as risk, cost, and political advantage peculiar to the Soviet side of the equation, have obviously sufficed to date to prevent a Soviet attack on China, and it is likely to continue to suffice in the future. It is impossible to isolate and measure with any precision the influence on Soviet calculations of any single factor in the total range of considerations, the American one included. It does seem reasonable to believe, however, that the new Sino-American relationship has created a significant uncertainty in Moscow as to what the American reaction would be in the event of a Soviet attack on China. This was especially true for about the first two years after the sensational first Kissinger visit to Peking in July 1971. Since about 1973 the effect of the Sino-American relationship on Soviet thinking has tended to wear off somewhat, but it has not shrunk to the point of being negligible.

The second major Chinese concern in cultivating a better relationship with the United States has been progress toward the "liberation" of Taiwan. From its own point of view, Peking was being quite accurate in describing Taiwan, during the months preceding the summit conference of February 1972 with President Nixon, as the "critical" issue in Sino-American relations, the one of the greatest intrinsic political importance to the Chinese side. This was an important matter, if for no other reason than because the radicals in Peking objected fundamentally to the opening to the United States and could probably not have been persuaded to acquiesce to it—Soviet threat or no Soviet threat—if they had not become convinced, or been told authoritatively by the chairman, that it promised gains on the Taiwan question. Given the changed climate of opinion on China in the United States and the American need felt for an opening to the PRC in order to help cope with the Soviet Union and Vietnam, Chou En-lai was probably able to argue persuasively that a better relationship with the United States would yield dividends in the direction of Taiwan. There was furthermore a respectable precedent, the period in the mid-1950s when Peking had tried to advance toward the "liberation" of Taiwan by means of contacts with the United States.

The third major consideration was probably trade and above all technological contact with the United States. It is predominantly at the two opposite ends of the spectrum of technological sophistication that the United States is an attractive trading partner: grain and cotton at one end, high technology equipment at the other. The PRC is a frequent importer, or would-be importer, in both categories. Its interest in the United States as a potential trading partner was probably heightened by the fact that after the Soviet Communist Party's Twenty-Fourth Congress (March 1971), Moscow intensified its own efforts to increase trade with the United States, as well as to promote what it understands by détente. In the Chinese case, an interest in trade with the United States unavoidably carried political overtones and presupposed an effort at détente, since the United States retained down to 1969 its politically motivated embargo on any trade by American citizens with the PRC.

Cambodia

Peking was politically close to Prince Norodom Sihanouk of Cambodia, a fact that was made clear when he was granted asylum in the PRC after his overthrow in mid-March 1970. Peking probably suspected, although incorrectly, that the United States had been involved in his overthrow, and in any case an adverse impact on any possibility of a Sino-American détente was guaranteed when at the end of April President Nixon ordered American ground forces to join South Vietnamese troops in a shallow incursion into Cambodia with the mission of cleaning out the North Vietnamese "sanctuaries" in that area.

In addition to launching a wave of anti-American propaganda and demonstrations, on May 19 Peking cancelled a Sino-American ambassadorial talk scheduled for the following day. On May 20, Mao Tse-tung issued a personal statement, the latest and strongest in a series that he had made at intervals since 1963, in condemnation of American (not Soviet) domestic politics and foreign policy. In vigorous language he condemned the alleged overthrow of Sihanouk by the United States and characteristically urged what would have amounted to a general revolutionary offensive by the Third World against American "imperialism," but without committing the PRC to any specific action.[16] Mao and his fellow-radicals were no doubt heartened by the storm of protest that the American incursion into Cambodia evoked in many parts of the world, including the United States itself.

Whatever Mao may have thought, however, it must have been obvious to Chou En-lai and some of his colleagues that the Cambodian crisis was a temporary affair with no essential bearing on the basic problems facing the PRC, notably the threat from the Soviet Union and the consequent need for some improvement in China's relations with the United States. Progress in that direction, however, clearly required some initiative from the American side that would counteract to some extent in the minds of the radicals the impact of the fall of Sihanouk and the incursion into Cambodia.

Appraising the Nixon Doctrine

During this period Peking undoubtedly thought of Vietnam in the way in which it was later to describe it, as the "urgent" issue in Sino-American relations. In other words, regardless of the Nixon administration's intentions on this score, and by implication regardless even of the Soviet threat, Peking was unwilling to enter into a positive relationship with the United States until the American withdrawal implied in the Nixon Doctrine had progressed to the point where Peking (including the radicals) could regard it as genuine and irreversible. This was evidently a point of principle, or what used to be called national honor, with Peking. One reason for this was that the American intervention in Vietnam had always had strong although somewhat vague anti-Chinese overtones, and Peking therefore regarded the prospective withdrawal with some reason as implying at least a partial abandonment of the tradition of American hostility to the PRC. More concretely, withdrawal from Vietnam, and the Nixon Doctrine as a whole, suggested an imminent end to what Peking had perceived as an American strategy of bullying and threatening the PRC, a strategy that had to be terminated before Peking's self-respect would permit it to initiate a positive relationship with the United States. The perception of the United States as ceasing its bullying and threatening of the PRC was no doubt enhanced in Peking's eyes by President Nixon's action in the second half of 1969 in easing the restrictions on American trade with and travel to the mainland of China and ending the Seventh Fleet's Taiwan Strait patrol.

From Peking's point of view, even the American incursion into Cambodia was not entirely a bad thing, since one of its main announced purposes was to protect and facilitate the withdrawal of American forces from the Mekong Delta. Furthermore, President Nixon had promised that American ground units would remain in Cambodia for only 60 days, and in fact they withdrew on schedule, at the end of June.

A further note encouraging to Peking was struck on July 1, when President Nixon told correspondent Howard K. Smith that he wanted to improve relations with the PRC as a means of coping with the Soviet Union (Washington Post, 1970).

All this evidently made it possible for Chou En-lai to begin the process of resuming the tentative opening to the United States that had been interrupted in early 1969, and again in May 1970. On July 10, 1970, Peking released an American Catholic bishop who had been in prison since 1958, clearly as a signal to the United States. In August the American journalist Edgar Snow, a friend of many years standing of the top Chinese leaders, was invited to China for what turned out to be a six month visit, in the course of which he interviewed Mao Tse-tung and Chou En-lai and stood next to Mao on the reviewing stand during the National Day parade (October 1) (Snow, 1971a).

In August-September, at an important meeting of the Chinese Communist Party's Central Committee (the so-called Second Plenum), the radical wing of the party, then led by Defense Minister Lin Piao, lost on several critical issues, one of which evidently was policy toward the United States. Lin and his supporters apparently opposed to one degree or another the opening to the United States advocated by Chou En-lai; since they lost, it must be assumed that Mao sided with Chou. Shortly after the meeting, Peking began to respond privately, through a variety of channels, to the American overtures that it had been receiving through similar channels since early 1969 (Taylor, 1974: 159-160). One of these channels was Edgar Snow, whom Mao told on December 18, 1970, that "at present the problems between China and the U.S.A. would have to be solved with Nixon. Mao would be happy to talk with him, either as a tourist or as President." Snow (1971b) also learned during that period that the American determination to withdraw from Vietnam was coming to be accepted in Peking as a fact.

In late February and early March 1971, South Vietnamese troops entered southern Laos briefly. Peking was evidently impressed, in private, by the fact that although this operation had American air support no American ground forces were involved. Evidently President Nixon was still serious about withdrawing American ground forces, whose presence had always worried Peking more than that of the other services, from Indochina.

Ping Pong Diplomacy

Less important, but still of some significance to Peking, was the fact that in mid-March 1971 the Nixon administration removed the last remaining restrictions on travel by Americans to the PRC. The significance was partly symbolic but it was also real, especially from the viewpoint of the Chinese radicals, be-cause it was now possible to invite to the PRC Americans who might exert an influence on public opinion that was favorable to Peking's interests.

The first such Americans to be invited after the lifting of the restrictions were a table tennis team then in Japan, who went to China in April accompanied by a group of American correspondents. This celebrated visit was followed by similar ones in both directions (New York Times, 1971; Topping, 1972). A substantial proportion of the Americans invited at first were leftists already sympathetic to the PRC (Committee of Concerned Asian Scholars, 1972). These were probably the only people-to-people contacts of which the radicals in Peking approved at that time. Chou En-lai's moderate coalition almost certainly placed less stock in them but promoted them mainly in the hope of easing the radicals' evident opposition to dealing with the U.S. government.

The First Kissinger Visit

One of the most important third-country intermediaries be-
tween Washington and Peking was President Nicolae Ceausesco of
Romania, who visited the United States in October 1970 and the
PRC in June 1971. Another was President Mohammed Yahya
Khan of Pakistan, a country that was important to both parties to
the emerging Sino-American relationship and was soon to become
more so in the course of the Indo-Pakistani war that gave birth to
Bangla Desh.

Partly as a result of their efforts, Presidential Assistant Henry
A. Kissinger succeeded in getting Chinese permission to visit
Peking secretly from July 9 to 15, 1971. The extreme secrecy
preserved during this trip was due to the sensitivity of the
Sino-American relationship in the domestic politics and foreign
relations of both countries, especially with the Soviet Union in
the case of the PRC and with Japan in the case of the United
States. Kissinger's talks with Chou En-lai were essentially explora-
tory, the main single topic being the possibility of a visit to the
PRC by President Nixon. Neither the Soviet Union nor the
question of Peking's possible admission to the United Nations
appears to have been discussed in any detail, the former presumably because it was too sensitive and the latter because it did
not seem important enough at that time.[17]

On July 15 the secrecy was lifted, and the world was astounded
to hear that Kissinger had just visited the PRC and that President
Nixon had been invited to do the same early the following year.

About that time the U.S. government began to plan its strategy on the Chinese representation question at the next session of
the United Nations General Assembly. The decision was to push
for a "two Chinas" approach, or in other words the admission of
the PRC without the expulsion of the Republic of China. Peking
indicated that this formula was still unacceptable, and that it
would not enter the United Nations as long as Taipei continued
to be seated in it. On the other hand, Peking did not make an
issue of this problem with the United States because it had more
important things on its mind and realized that the U.S. freedom
of maneuver in this respect was limited. As it turned out, Peking's

supporters at the United Nations were able to bring about its admission and the simultaneous expulsion of the Republic of China on October 25, 1971, while Kissinger was visiting the PRC for the second time.

The Anti-Japanese Campaign

Beginning in the spring of 1970, Peking launched a massive propaganda campaign against the government of Japanese Premier Sato. When American visitors to China talked to Chinese officials the following year, they were subjected to this campaign, in the form of statements that Japan was remilitarizing and was embarking once more on a campaign of overseas expansion (Reston, 1971). The reasons for these allegations, whose absurdity was certainly known to many leaders in Peking including Chou En-lai, are probably several in number. Two are relevant to the United States.

One was a desire to capitalize on the serious strains in Japanese-American relations during 1971, the so-called Nixon shocks, one of the most important of which was the decision to send Kissinger to Peking without informing the Japanese government in advance. More specifically, Peking probably hoped to reinforce the Nixon administration's apparent strong anti-Japanese bias and by contrast to portray the PRC, rather than Japan, as the most reliable partner of the United States in the Far East.

The other consideration, more subtle, related to the need to rationalize Peking's opening to the United States in a way that might help to overcome the objections of the radicals, of whom the most important apart from Mao himself was Lin Piao. The argument ran to the effect that since Japan was now once more the main threat to China and the rest of Asia, it made sense to cooperate temporarily with the lesser adversary, the United States, which was also seemingly on bad terms with Japan.[18] The real point, of course, was to collaborate with the United States against the Soviet Union, but this was evidently less appealing to the radicals and was certainly provocative to Moscow and accordingly not suitable for public discussion. The plausibility of this interpretation is enhanced by the fact that shortly after the fall and death of Lin Piao, the leading opponent of the opening to the United States, in September 1971, Peking's anti-Japanese propaganda campaign began to taper off, presumably at least partly because it was no longer so useful (Shinkichi, 1972: 4).

The Fall of Lin Piao

Like the anti-Japanese propaganda campaign, the fall of Lin Piao had important aspects that were not directly relevant to Sino-American relations and that need not be discussed here.

There is little doubt that Lin and his close colleague, Chief of Staff Huang Yung-sheng, who fell together with him, opposed the opening to the United States, whatever their attitude toward the Soviet Union and other matters may have been.[19] Even the Kissinger visit and the announcement of the invitation to President Nixon apparently did not put an end to their opposition. While the crisis culminating in their fall on September 11-12 was in progress, there was considerable nervousness in Washington as to whether the invitation to President Nixon was still valid.[20] But by October 5, when it was announced that Kissinger would visit Peking again later that month, all concerned must have realized that it was. The October visit was devoted largely to making definite arrangements for the presidential visit, including the date.

5. THE NIXON SUMMIT

In playing host to President Nixon, Peking was taking a step that not only marked a departure from its conventional foreign policy but was politically controversial, more so in China probably than it was in the United States. The extremely tight and effective security precautions with which Peking surrounded the visit, which testified to a re-emergence of the security police since the Cultural Revolution without which a presidential visit would have been unthinkable, were designed not only to protect the visitor but to isolate him from ordinary Chinese and thereby minimize charges by the radicals that the visit was exerting a corrupting political influence. The low-key greeting at the airport and the absence of crowds at that time served a similar purpose, in addition to cooling the president's ebullience and putting him on his best behavior. But once Chou En-lai had satisfied himself of his guest's sincerity and seriousness, it became desirable to lend authoritative dignity to the visit in order to fend off the objections of the radicals. This could be done only by Mao Tse-tung, who accordingly received Nixon on the afternoon of the first day of the visit (February 21, 1972), earlier than had been expected; the conversation dealt with the topics to be covered in the negotiations, but mainly in general terms.[21]

Background Considerations

As already indicated, Peking's main single purpose in inviting President Nixon, and in conducting its opening to the United States as a whole, was to improve its maneuvering and bargaining position with respect to the Soviet Union and diminish the likelihood of a Soviet attack on China. This was an extremely sensitive subject, for two main reasons. In the first place, Moscow was fully aware of Peking's purpose and very concerned about it; there was therefore a possibility, at least in the Chinese view, that public indications that this was indeed the main purpose of the invitation to Nixon might evoke some sort of Soviet retaliation, which was exactly what Peking was trying to avoid. Secondly, the Nixon administration was deeply committed to a détente with the Soviet Union, and the president was scheduled to visit Moscow in the near future; he was accordingly eager to gain leverage on the Soviet Union from the Peking trip among other things, but not to allow his dealings with the Chinese to be conducted in such a way as to wreck his hopes for détente with Moscow. A related and significant point is that Chinese knowledge of the forthcoming Nixon visit to Moscow was one of the rather few levers that the president held in his hand in Peking; in some other respects he was critically vulnerable, or at least manipulable.

His Chinese hosts, and Chou En-lai above all, were keenly aware of these weaknesses. As it turned out, Chou played on them with great skill. For one thing, it was of course a presidential election year in the United States. Largely for this reason, the president's domestic affairs staff had insisted on maximum media coverage of the visit. The net effect of these considerations was that it would have been practically unthinkable for the president to bring home an obvious diplomatic failure; if concessions were needed to avoid such an outcome, he would have to make some. Secondly, the Chinese saw that their American counterparts were almost desperately eager for a settlement of the Vietnam conflict, preferably before the 1972 presidential election, and that they hoped that Peking would be helpful, or at least would give the appearance of being helpful, toward this end. Finally, the Chinese side realized that its American guests were not only affected by the usual China mystique and by a desire to visit Peking for its own sake, and not only had a typically American eagerness to establish "communication" and foster goodwill, but considered that the United States owed the PRC compensation for previous wrongs, including at least some aspects of American policy toward Taiwan, and were prepared to make concessions for those reasons.

The Negotiations

Because of the sensitivity already discussed, it is unlikely that the Soviet question played much of a role in the negotiations. Practically speaking, the two parties were not in a position to coordinate a program of joint action for coping with Moscow. The most that could be achieved at that time toward that end was to create a general perception that Sino-American relations were improving.

Similarly, the Chinese side did not say much about Indochina and Korea or press for a rapid American military withdrawal from those areas. Clearly Peking was reasonably well satisfied with current American policy in these respects, convinced that it no longer constituted a serious threat to Chinese security, and anxious not to allow these relatively peripheral issues to disrupt progress on more important ones. Indeed, there were some indications that Chou En-lai at least had begun to adopt a view that Peking was to make clear, although not formally or publicly, during the next few years: that the United States ought not to engage in further major military withdrawals from Asia, except for Indochina and presumably Taiwan, or for that matter from Europe, because to do so might create a "vacuum" that the Soviet Union might "fill" or otherwise exploit. In spite of its criticality the year before, the South Asian subcontinent does not appear to have played much of a role at the Peking summit. Nor, apparently, did Japan, in part because of American reluctance—in spite of the poor state of Japanese-American relations at that time—to go behind the back of the United States' principal Asian ally, and in part because of the fact that Peking's intense Japanophobia of the previous two years had begun to subside (Brandon, 1972: 195-196).

An obvious possibility that intrigued outside observers of the Peking summit was that of some sort of Taiwan-for-Vietnam deal (Evans and Novak, 1972). In other words, in exchange for American concessions on Taiwan, might Peking agree to put pressure on Hanoi, perhaps by cutting off military aid, in order to induce it to be more reasonable at the Paris talks? In reality, such a deal was out of the question. On the American side, there were self-imposed limits on the permissible concessions regarding Taiwan, and these concessions fell considerably short of meeting Peking's demands. On the Chinese side, Peking was unwilling to promise the United States to put pressure on Hanoi or to be actively helpful in any other way in the matter of a Vietnam settlement, for example by sponsoring another Geneva Conference. Peking was not prepared to run the risk of antagonizing Hanoi to the point of driving it into the arms of the Soviet Union, especially since Moscow on its side had similarly been rejecting American requests for help in arranging a Vietnam settlement. Chou En-lai reportedly told Nixon to address himself, not to Peking, but to the "revolutionary" leaders of Indochina including Sihanouk (Washington Post, 1972f, citing an interview by Wilfred Burchett with Sihanouk).

This does not mean that Peking and Moscow were not ready to be helpful in their own ways, meaning behind the scenes and not admittedly in response to American requests. Both were driven by a competitive urge for détente with the United States, as long as they did not unduly antagonize Hanoi. Peking for its part had already begun to reinforce the credibility of its claim to want better relations with the United States by moderating its behavior—not so much its propaganda—toward the three familiar trouble spots of East Asia: Korea, the Taiwan Strait, and Indochina. For example, at the time of the first Kissinger visit Peking had sent a delegate to the Military Armistice Commission in Korea, for the first time in five years (New York Times, 1971).

For obvious reasons, the most contentious and time-consuming issue dealt with by Chou and Nixon was Taiwan. Over the reported objections of one State Department member of the delegation, the American side agreed not to refer publicly during the conference to the U.S. ties with and commitments to the Republic of China. In return, Peking refrained from a public attack on American policy toward Taiwan for the duration of the conference and in the final communique. The American omission, and the very presence of the American delegation in Peking as contrasted with the lack of comparable visits to Taiwan, symbolized to Peking's satisfaction the fact that the United States had clearly come to rate its emerging relationship with the PRC as more important than its alliance with the Republic of China. On the other hand, as already indicated there were serious differences at the Peking summit over Taiwan. The American side refused to do, or promise formally to do, anything that would amount to an abandonment of Taiwan—in other words, a transfer of diplomatic relations from Taipei to Peking or a denunciation of the security treaty with the Republic of China—at any rate in the near future; the imminence of a political campaign and a presidential election was probably a factor in this refusal. The American side was prepared, nevertheless, to make certain less-than-drastic concessions on Taiwan for the sake of cultivating détente with Peking, and these were to appear in the final communique. Peking refused for its part, as it had been refusing since about 1955, to give a formal "renunciation of force" pledge with respect to Taiwan, even in private.

In spite of this, and in spite of the insistence by both sides after the conference that no secret agreements had been made, there appears to have been a tacit understanding that Peking would confine itself to political methods in working toward the "liberation" of Taiwan. A more and difficult and controversial question is whether the American side encouraged the Chinese side to believe that the United States would proceed to full "normalization," including diplomatic relations, at some appropriate time. In one of his banquet speeches (February 22), Chou En-lai said that the PRC and the United States should have "normal state relations on the basis of the five principles" of peaceful coexistence, in spite of the "great differences" between them. There is no question, then, about the Chinese desire for "normalization," and Peking was to say later that it had been promised eventual "normalization" by Nixon and Kissinger. The uncertainty is obviously about the American response: it appears to have been, both publicly and in private, the rather unheroic one of endorsing "normalization" while remaining calculatedly vague as to whether the meaning of that term included full diplomatic relations, and insisting quite sensibly that the main need was for Peking and Taipei to settle their differences in one way or another, other than by force.

The Shanghai Communique

The text of the final statement, known as the Shanghai Communique, was negotiated at length and with great care. The differences between the two sides were serious enough so that a joint communique that simply ignored them in the interest of presenting an appearance of harmony would have been a meaningless and even ridiculous document. It was agreed that this approach should be avoided and that the communique should deal fairly frankly with the differences, and yet in a way not likely to endanger the developing détente. This was achieved by having each side state where its individual positions differed from those of the other side, but in a relatively moderate way. In fact, each side was allowed to go over the other side's positions in advance and indicate objections. Each side therefore had something close to a veto over the other's input to the communique.

As a result of this procedure, the Shanghai Communique, which was issued on February 27 just before the conclusion of the visit, contained three main sections: one that stated agreed positions, one that stated unilateral Chinese positions, one that stated unilateral American positions. The order in which this was done was rather cumbersome and disjointed and will not be followed here; instead, the summary given below arranges the issues dealt with in what seems to be a logical order and indicates the position, or divergent positions, expressed on each issue.

With regard to the general principles to govern bilateral Sino-American relations, the two sides agreed as follows: There was to be further progress toward "normalization" (which was not defined), including an expansion of scientific and cultural exchange and trade. Sino-American relations were to be based on the "five principles of peaceful coexistence" (which were not labeled as such), the third of which abjures interference in the internal affairs of other countries and could be interpreted by Peking as a self-denying pledge by the United States with respect to Taiwan; it is interesting, and indicative of the new American mood, that down to that time the United States had consistently refused to endorse the "five principles." The two sides agreed to remain in contact with each other; a senior American representative was to visit Peking from time to time—no senior PRC official would visit the United States as long as there was an embassy of the Republic of China in Washington—for "concrete consultations to further the normalization of relations."

On Taiwan, the Chinese side asserted, not for the first time, that it was the "crucial question obstructing the normalization of relations" between the PRC and the United States; that Taiwan was a province of China and no one could legitimately interfere with its "liberation;" that American troops and bases must be withdrawn from the island (no time limit was specified); and that no separate status of any kind for Taiwan was permissible. The American side stated that it did not "challenge" this position, which it attributed to all Chinese on both sides of the Taiwan Strait (denying even the existence of the Taiwan independence movement), that there is only one China and that Taiwan is part of it. The American side urged a peaceful settlement on the two parties involved; on the understanding that the trend was in that direction, the United States would ultimately withdraw all its military personnel and bases from the island. "In the meantime, it will progressively reduce its forces and military installations on Taiwan as the tension in the area diminishes." In other words, the United States was making its military withdrawal conditional on the PRC's continued good behavior not only in the Taiwan Strait but in the rest of Asia, as well as on the general growth of international stability in the region.

The communique dealt with a number of third countries of interest to the two parties. On Vietnam, the Chinese side endorsed the Provisional Revolutionary Government of South Vietnam's seven-point program of July 1, 1971, which demanded an end to American political support for the Thieu government as well as other things; the American side came out for a political settlement for Indochina without outside interference but stated that even in the absence of such a settlement the United States would ultimately withdraw its forces from Indochina with due regard for the self-determination of its peoples. On Korea, the Chinese side endorsed the North Korean proposal of April 12, 1971, on "peaceful unification," which demanded among other things an American military withdrawal from South Korea and the abolition of the United Nations Commission for the Unification and Rehabilitation of Korea; the American side reiterated its support for the Republic of Korea and for the latter's efforts at relaxation of tension in the peninsula. On Japan, the Chinese side expressed opposition to Japanese militarism, without making clear whether the reference was to an actual or to a potential situation; the American side stated that it placed the "highest value on its friendly relations with Japan" and would continue to cultivate them. On South Asia, both sides favored the maintenance of the ceasefire between India and Pakistan; the Chinese side expressed support for self-determination for Kashmir, or in other words, for a plebiscite as demanded by Pakistan; neither side mentioned Bangla Desh, a sore subject for both.

With respect to international relations in general, the Chinese side declared itself for liberation and revolution for "all oppressed people and nations" and the withdrawal of all troops from foreign soil (including by implication, as Peking made clear on other occasions, Soviet troops from the Mongolian People's Republic). The American side proclaimed its support for peace, individual liberties, and the development of "communications between countries that have different ideologies." Both sides agreed that they would not negotiate (with each other and presumably with other countries as well) on behalf of third parties and would not reach understandings directed against third parties (presumably a reassurance to the Soviet Union and the Republic of China, for the most part). Both sides declared themselves opposed to spheres of influence, for themselves as well as for others. Both sides agreed that "neither should seek hegemony in the Asia-Pacific region and each is opposed to the efforts by any other country or group of countries to establish such hegemony." Occasional later statements to the effect that this "anti-hegemony" clause was inserted at American initiative notwithstanding, considerable evidence, including another passage in the Shanghai Communique, makes it clear that the actual initiative was Chinese, and that the clause was directed against the Soviet Union.

The Peking summit and the Shanghai Communique may not have changed the world, as President Nixon claimed that they did, but they certainly moved the Sino-American relationship noticeably in the direction desired by both sides. Objectively speaking, Peking appears to have come out considerably the better of the two parties. Unlike the American side, it had made no observable concessions, apart from the invitation to President Nixon itself.

6. THE ROCKY ROAD TO NORMALIZATION

In the wake of the Peking summit and the Shanghai Communique, each party was clearly serious in desiring "normalization," or in other words the best attainable state of Sino-American relations consistent with the promotion of its own interests. Just as the American side had to insist that it had not sold out Taipei, so the Chinese side had to insist that it had not sold out Hanoi; each was correct, at least from its own point of view. But even more important, perhaps, in Peking's eyes was the fact that a Soviet-American summit was due in late May. Peking regarded this prospect with the same degree of enthusiasm with which Moscow had regarded the Peking summit, which is to say none at all.

Peking and the Indochina Agreements

Chou En-lai is believed to have visited Hanoi secretly on March 3-5, 1972, and to have held talks with the North Vietnamese leadership on matters that included the problem of political coordination among the elements of the Indochinese left; he also reportedly reassured Hanoi that he had not compromised its interests during his talks with President Nixon, for example by agreeing to mediate the Indochina war (New York Times, 1972f). All this appears plausible, but it does not account for the secrecy of the trip; Chou had made announced visits to Hanoi as recently as September 1969 and March 1971. But the secrecy would be understandable on the hypothesis that, in the hope of disrupting or at least complicating the approaching Soviet-American summit conference as well as improving relations with Hanoi, Chou gave assent to a major military offensive already contemplated by Hanoi but did not want the assent to become known, because the knowledge might endanger the new Sino-American détente and in particular the prospect of American withdrawal from Taiwan.[22]

Hanoi's massive Easter offensive, which was launched on March 30, appears to have had Soviet as well as logistical support (Washington Post, 1972e). In view of Moscow's anxiety to hold its scheduled summit with President Nixon, if only because Peking had already done the same, and of the Soviet eagerness not to endanger the pending ratification by the West German Bundestag of Moscow's friendship treaty with Bonn signed in 1970, it must be assumed that Hanoi exerted strong pressure for support on Moscow as well as on Peking. The initial public Chinese reaction to the offensive and to the resulting resumption of American bombing of North Vietnam was relatively subdued. The mining of Haiphong harbor, announced by President Nixon on May 8, was too spectacular to be ignored; Peking denounced the mining loudly, while remaining silent on the invasion of South Vietnam that had provoked it (text of Chinese statement in New York Times, 1972e).

A merely declaratory policy was obviously not enough if Peking was to avoid alienating Hanoi. Accordingly, on May 19 in talks with Soviet, Mongolian, and North Vietnamese representatives, Peking agreed to cooperate, within the framework of an agreement signed on April 30, 1965, in transshipping by rail an increased volume of Soviet, as well as Chinese (presumably) military equipment to North Vietnam (New York Times, 1972d). On the other hand, Peking appears to have cited its security considerations as a basis for refusing to allow Soviet vessels bound for North Vietnam to use Chinese ports (New York Times, 1972c; Washington Post, 1972c, 1972d); Peking may have wanted not to be held responsible by the United States for taking part in an effort to break the blockade of Haiphong.

Peking was undoubtedly disappointed that neither the United States nor the Soviet Union allowed the crisis in Vietnam, serious though it was, to disrupt the Moscow summit. Once the damage, such as it was, had been done, Peking allowed its interest in improved relations with the United States to come to the fore again. This meant that it became more favorable, or at least began to appear more favorable, than it had been until recently to the idea of settlements for the Indochina countries, with the qualification that it still wanted to avoid alienating its allies, including Sihanouk (Salisbury, 1972). Consistent with this last requirement, Peking appears to have agreed at some time in July to allow Soviet ships to make limited use of certain South China ports (Kun, 1972).

The resumption of American bombing of North Vietnam in December 1972—after an interval during which it seemed that "peace was at hand," in Dr. Kissinger's famous phrase—created another problem for Peking. Its response was severely, and predictably, critical. (Comments by Chou En-lai as reported in New York Times, 1972a; Washington Post, 1972a). On the other hand, Peking was evidently growing increasingly tired of Hanoi's propensity to escalate, which both endangered the Sino-American détente and increased North Vietnam's dependence on the Soviet Union for heavy military equipment. Furthermore, the fact that since May China had been the only accessible route for Communist military equipment bound for North Vietnam, apart from a Soviet air route of limited capacity across India and Laos, posed an obviously increased threat to the Sino-American détente in the event that the United States chose to make an issue of it. For roughly these reasons, during the last months of 1972, Peking as well as Moscow appear to have applied various forms of pressure to Hanoi behind the scenes, probably short of a threat to cut off the flow of arms, in an effort to render it more accommodating at the conference table, much as the United States was doing to Saigon. These pressures evidently contributed, or at any rate they were later credited by high American officials with having contributed, to the ultimate signing of the Paris Agreement on South

Vietnam on January 23, 1973 (Christian Science Monitor, 1972; Washington Post, 1972b; 1973d; New York Times, 1973e). Within a few months, both Peking and Moscow appear to have reduced the flow of arms to Hanoi significantly (New York Times, 1973c; Washington Star-News, 1973). In their official view, as well as that of the United States, the war in Vietnam, meaning in reality the active role of the external powers in it, was over.

The United States was sufficiently eager for a comparable ceasefire in Laos so that its allies, the Royal Laotian Government under Premier Souvanna Phouma, felt compelled to sign a highly disadvantageous ceasefire and political agreement with its opponents, the communist-dominated Pathet Lao, on February 20, 1973. During the diplomatic maneuvering that accompanied the working out of this agreement, the United States and its Laotian friends found themselves supported, at least behind the scenes, by the PRC, the Pathet Lao being supported by Hanoi and the Soviet Union.[23]

In Cambodia there was of course no agreement. The PRC took a consistently hostile line toward American support for the Lon Nol government in Phnom Penh, not only because Peking was strongly committed to Sihanouk and through him to the so-called Khmer Rouge, but because the Cambodian left shared with Peking a strong, although largely unpublicized, antipathy to Hanoi and to the possibility of North Vietnamese domination of Cambodia. The steady decline and ultimate collapse of the Lon Nol government following the Congressionally enforced cessation of American bombing in Cambodia on August 15, 1973, had the effect, however, of removing the country as a serious issue in Sino-American relations. Peking refused an American request to help arrange the release of the *Mayaguez,* but it may have urged Phnom Penh behind the scenes to let the ship go.

Establishment of the Liaison Offices

The signing of the Paris Agreement had a sharply beneficial effect on Sino-American relations. From the Chinese point of view, this was entirely logical inasmuch as Peking had previously described the American military involvement in Vietnam as the "urgent" issue hampering an improvement of Sino-American relations.

For both substantive and symbolic reasons, a more effective channel of communication than the occasional visits to Peking of a senior American representative mentioned in the Shanghai Communique was obviously desirable. A series of talks between the two parties' ambassadors to Paris during 1972 was also clearly inadequate, although helpful. And yet the American commitment to the Republic of China continued to prevent the establishment of full diplomatic relations between Peking and Washington. A way needed to be found around this obstacle, and one was found.

On February 15, 1973, Kissinger arrived in Peking for his fifth visit. The champagne atmosphere of the Paris Agreement still lingered, and for the first time (except when accompanying President Nixon) he was received by Mao Tse-tung; he also held talks with Chou En-lai. The main business of the visit was an agreement to establish a "liaison office," or in other words an embassy in everything but name, in each capital, in the interest of "accelerating the normalization of relations" as the communique put it.[24] The liaison offices were set up during the next few months; the American one in Peking received extraordinarily good cooperation from the Chinese side.[25] The United States Liaison Office was headed by David Bruce, a distinguished diplomat of ambassadorial rank, who arrived in May. The Chinese Liaison Office in Washington was headed by Huang Chen, who had also held ambassadorial appointments and was a member of the Chinese Communist Party's Central Committee. The important thing about the liaison offices was not the business they transacted, which was generally routine, but the simple fact that they existed, both in case of urgent need and as symbols of the improving state of Sino-American relations.

Economic Contacts and Issues

Given the PRC's interest in importing American food grains, fiber, and high technology equipment, the eagerness of American firms to sell on the China market, and the limited demand for

Chinese goods in the United States, it was inevitable that Sino-American trade should be heavily unbalanced in favor of the United States.

In an effort to do what it could to maximize its exports to the United States, Peking invited 42 American businessmen to the spring 1972 Canton Trade Fair, of whom something over 30 actually attended; they were shown great consideration.[26] There was a growing American attendance at later Canton Trade Fairs.

Late in 1972 the PRC initiated an ambitious program of importing high technology equipment, including whole plants, to a total amount of about $2.5 billion. The main categories were steel, petrochemicals, chemical fertilizers, and electric power generating equipment. In spite of its horror of debt and its emphasis on "self-reliance," Peking entered extensively into what it preferred to call deferred payment arrangements, which in effect involved credits (Eckstein, 1975: 140, 148-149). As a step toward paying for these imports, the PRC sharply increased the prices of its exports in 1973.

Some large contracts were signed with American firms during this period. They included contracts covering 10 Boeing 707 jet transports ($150 million), eight ammonia plants from the M. W. Kellogg Company of Houston ($215 million), and satellite communications equipment from RCA, (Clarke and Avery, 1975: 515). Orders for American wheat began to be placed by Peking in 1972 (New York Times, 1972b).

As a result of transactions such as these, the total volume of Sino-American trade both ways rose from a negligible figure in 1971 to $95.9 million in 1972, $805.1 million in 1973, and $933.8 million in 1974 (Clarke and Avery, 1975: 512). Peking was understandably concerned, however, at the heavy imbalance in favor of the United States (roughly seven to one in 1974).[27] In 1974 the PRC incurred an international payments deficit estimated on the order of $1 billion. For this reason, and probably also because of smut that had been present in some wheat imported from the United States and because of generally good Chinese harvests, Peking cancelled early in 1975 orders for American wheat totaling about one million tons (New York Times, 1975g). Partly for this reason, Sino-American trade fell in 1975 to a total volume estimated at $400 million, the imbalance in favor of the United States being approximately five to three (Clarke and Avery, 1975: 512). On the bright side, from the Chinese point of view, there was the fact that in 1975 Chinese cotton textile exports to the United States rose sharply, to a position among foreign suppliers of the American market second only to that of Hong Kong (New York Times, 1976a).

Chinese exports to the United States, as well as to other countries, were adversely affected by a variety of factors, including of course "slumpflation" in the developed countries and the effects of worldwide raw material price increases. But there was a specific and serious problem in the case of Chinese exports to the United States, namely the lack of most-favored-nation status, without which many types of Chinese commodities were charged much higher import duties than would otherwise have been the case. The PRC's lack of most-favored-nation status in the United States was due in part to the absence of a Sino-American commercial agreement, which was partly due in turn to Peking's reluctance, for ideological and political reasons, to sign formal agreements with the U.S. government. There was another obstacle as well: the failure of the two sides, even after a series of negotiations that began in February 1973 at the foreign ministers level (New York Times, 1973b), to settle the matter of private American claims (totaling about $200 million) of compensation for assets nationalized by the PRC and blocked Chinese assets (totaling about $78 million) in the United States. The inability of the two sides to reach agreement on these questions appears to be due mainly to Peking's attitude, which is probably influenced by the imbalance in favor of the United States and by the reluctance already mentioned to conclude government-to-government agreements with the United States (Luther, 1975: 213-222).

One of the most interesting and potentially important problems in Sino-American economic relations is that of possible future Chinese exports of petroleum products to the United States.[28] Since 1959 major deposits have been found, the most important to date being located in Manchuria (the Taching field) and near the North China coast. So far Peking has not shown an active interest in exporting oil to the United States, although it has begun to do so to several Asian countries including Japan, and it has rejected approaches from several American oil companies interested in providing technical assistance, entering into joint ventures, and so forth. Roughly the same is true of oil deposits on China's continental shelf, with the difference that the existence of large offshore oil reserves is fairly widely assumed but is not yet proved through drilling. The main reason for this is that the PRC is not yet in a mood or position to explore and develop offshore oil for itself (except for some deposits close inshore in the Pohai Gulf), has ideological and political inhibitions about cooperating in any way with foreign oil companies, and yet by loudly asserting since December 1970 its claim to control all resources on the continental shelf has prevented foreign oil companies and nearby Asian governments from doing much in the way of exploration. On the other hand, the obvious financial incentives involved appear likely to outweigh Peking's reservations in the long run. Japan will probably remain the main purchaser and beneficiary of Chinese oil exports, whether from onshore or offshore reserves, but not the only one. For one thing, in spite of its nervousness over its current dependence on Middle Eastern oil Japan will probably be unwilling to exchange this for dependence on the PRC. For another the PRC seems committed to a policy of conducting a significant, if fluctuating, level of trade with the United States, and in this connection oil has obvious and powerful attractions (Li, 1975: 143-162; Park, 1975: 27-46; 1973: 212-260; Harrison, 1975: 3-27; Park and Cohen, 1975: 28-49).

The Korean Question

Although the PRC probably feels fewer reservations about the idea of peaceful unification of Korea under Pyongyang than it has felt about the idea of even peaceful unification of Vietnam under Hanoi, the point is academic since there is no likelihood of such an outcome in Korea under present conditions. The only possible route to Korean unification is through war, and Peking is clearly and strongly opposed to that eventuality because of the likelihood that it would become involved by virtue of its alliance with North Korea dating from 1961. Since the presence of American forces in South Korea is clearly a stabilizing factor, the PRC almost certainly does not want them withdrawn, although for the sake of its relations with North Korea it says from time to time that it does. Peking's opposition to the idea of another war in the Korean peninsula is shared by the other powers concerned, with the possible exception of the two Koreas themselves. On the other hand, Peking tries to avoid alienating Pyongyang, much as it tries to avoid alienating Hanoi, if only in order not to drive it into the arms of Moscow.

These considerations were all discernible in the Chinese statements made at the time of Kim Il Song's most recent visit to Peking (April 18-26, 1975), from which he took home a small political plum in the form of an affirmation by the Chinese side, for the first time, that it regarded Pyongyang as the only legal government in the Korean peninsula. On military matters, on the other hand, Peking appears to have made no significant commitments to additional support for North Korea (Hinton, 1973b: 15-27; Hinton, 1975b: 25-51).

Since the existence of the military ties between the United States and the Republic of Korea is not dependent on that of the United Nations Command in Korea, Peking can and does curry favor with Pyongyang by demanding the abolition of the United Nations Command, in the knowledge that by doing so it is not endangering Korean stability. It does not neglect to assert, in addition, that the Soviet Union is not really interested in the abolition of the United Nations Command. Such was the line that Peking took, loudly as usual, at the fall 1975 session of the General Assembly (Koh, 1976: 43-63).

The record of the PRC's recent Korean policy, in short, shows a characteristically clear recognition of risks where they exist, a primary concern (after its own security) for its new relationship with the United States, and a secondary although not insignificant concern for its older ties with Pyongyang. It is not clear that, under the circumstances, the United States could ask for much more.

Peking and the Soviet-American Détente

For many years Peking has claimed that the Soviet-American relationship embodied both elements of "contention" and elements of "collusion," in proportions that varied over time. There have apparently been differences within the Chinese leadership on this, the more ideologically inclined leaders (or radicals) emphasizing the "collusion" aspect, the moderates such as Chou En-lai emphasizing the "contention" aspect.

For the past few years, Chinese leaders (Teng Hsiao-p'ing, 1974) have stated that a war between the United States and the Soviet Union (that is, World War III) will occur "some day," unless it is prevented by the implicitly more likely alternative eventuality of a more or less worldwide revolution, apparently in the United States and the Soviet Union themselves as well as elsewhere. This "prediction" is so ideological, so Maoist, and so qualified that it is almost meaningless as an indication of anything but the propaganda line that Peking chooses to put forth at home and abroad because it is acceptable to the radicals. It certainly does not establish the truth of the frequent Soviet charges that the PRC is trying to incite a Soviet-American war (Henry, 1974: 129-139). The PRC would run serious risks in the course of such a war and almost certainly does not want one, whatever its propaganda may suggest. Similar caution should be used in interpreting Peking's occasional statements since 1973 that the main thrust of Soviet "expansion" is not toward China but in some other direction, usually said to be Europe. Such statements have ulterior motives, including a desire to prevent the United States and other Western countries from relaxing their vigilance against the Soviet Union on the assumption that it is the PRC that is absorbing the main thrust of Soviet "expansion."

Even though Peking does not really desire a Soviet-American war, it has serious reservations about Soviet-American détente, in view of its bad relations with the Soviet Union and its hopes for the United States as a counterweight against possible Soviet pressures on China. In particular, Peking is worried by the fact that the United States has allowed the Soviet Union to achieve approximate strategic parity and has in effect institutionalized this new and significant relationship in the SALT agreements. In short, Peking, like many others, tends to believe that the United States has lost the will to hold up its end of the Cold War with the Soviet Union, with results that may ultimately be seriously adverse not only for the United States but for other countries including the PRC. Peking certainly believes that, whatever Secretary Kissinger and other Americans may say about "equidistance," the United States in practice places a higher priority on its relations with the Soviet Union than on its relations with the PRC. A good example of the kind of evidence leading Peking to this conclusion is a provision in the Helsinki Agreement (Part 2, Section I) to the effect that participating states must give advance notice of military maneuvers near their borders, unless the maneuvering power's territory extends beyond Europe and the border is shared with a "non-European non-participating State" (U.S. Department of State, 1975: 85). The exclusion obviously covers Soviet maneuvers near the Chinese border, and the United States is of course a signatory to the Helsinki Agreement.

Peking appears to fear that it is considered by the United States to be so immobilized at present by its quarrel with the Soviet Union that it can be taken for granted and manipulated by the United States. On the other hand, Peking also perceives that there is some concern in the United States that the PRC and the Soviet Union might settle their differences. For these reasons it is to Peking's advantage to do something from time to time to shake the American belief in the current incurability of the Sino-Soviet dispute and to play on the contrasting American nervousness over the possibility of a Sino-Soviet rapprochement. It was probably with this in mind that Peking sent a relatively conciliatory message to Moscow on November 6, 1974, shortly before the Soviet-American summit conference at Vladivostok, and released three captured Soviet helicopter crewmen on December 27, 1975, not long after President Ford's visit to Peking.

Since about the time of the Vladivostok summit, Peking appears to have been increasingly concerned over the trends that it thought it perceived in Soviet-American relations, which were along the lines already indicated. This concern was clearly increased by the dismissal of Secretary of Defense James R. Schlesinger on November 2, 1975, and was reportedly expressed to Secretary Kissinger when he came to Peking the previous month in order to arrange the details of the Ford visit, as well as to President Ford himself early in December. The famous invitation to former President Nixon to visit the PRC again in February 1976, on the fourth anniversary of his earlier visit, was intended to demonstrate approval of his China policy, which Peking interprets as more pro-Chinese than President Ford's with respect to the Soviet Union as well as Taiwan.

Just as the anti-Soviet motivation was the most important single one for Peking's decision to cultivate better relations with the United States, so Peking's disappointment in this respect is probably the most serious single problem currently facing the Sino-American relationship. The radicals have always been skeptical about the opening to the United States and can be expected to make difficulties for it to the extent that they think there is reason to believe that "collusion" predominates over "contention" in Soviet-American relations; if that is so, they would argue, what is the controversial relationship with the United States doing for China to compensate for its ideological and emotional distastefulness (to them)?

Taiwan After the Shanghai Communique

Similarly, the radicals have almost certainly argued that the United States has not made enough concessions on Taiwan and has obviously not gone the whole distance by transferring diplomatic recognition to Peking and abrogating the security treaty with the Republic of China. Chou En-lai and his associates, on the other hand, have been willing to be patient on Taiwan in the interest of other considerations and have tried from time to time to silence radical pressures on the Taiwan question by suggesting that if deprived of American support the Nationalists might turn to a "third party," meaning the Soviet Union.

During the period after the Shanghai Communique, the United States reduced its military personnel and aircraft on Taiwan, but not to zero, and it not only maintained but in some ways strengthened its relationship with the Republic of China, for example by allowing it to open additional consulates on American territory and by selling the Republic of China increasingly advanced conventional military equipment. Peking regarded these developments, which were clearly influenced by continuing conservative support in the United States for the Republic of China and by the approach of the 1976 presidential election, as contrary to its understanding of "normalization" as promised in the Shanghai Communique, or in other words progress toward full diplomatic relations and a cutting of American diplomatic and military ties with the Republic of China. There is little doubt that these problems were raised in earnest terms by the Chinese during the Kissinger and Ford visits in 1975 (Washington Star, 1975a).

Nevertheless, Peking did not need to feel completely discontent with its progress on the Taiwan question. The United States had clearly indicated a priority for its new relationship with the PRC over its commitment to the Republic of China. For many years, no American president or secretary of state had visited Taiwan.

In the absence of more concrete steps toward the "liberation" of Taiwan through dealing with the United States, Peking continued to work toward that goal by trying to cultivate a feeling of helplessness on Taiwan and an interest in an accommodation with the mainland, by such things as releasing a number of elderly Nationalist "war criminals" from jail in 1975 and allowing them to leave the country.

An issue related to that of Taiwan was the growing Chinese assertiveness in the South China Sea. On January 20, 1974, Chinese forces drove some South Vietnamese units off the Paracel Islands and remained in occupation of them (New York Times, 1974g). Peking also claimed the Spratlys, several hundred miles farther south, but at least for the time being made no move to occupy them. In the fall of 1975, Peking conducted extensive naval maneuvers in the South China Sea (New York Times, 1976b). Although probably directed mainly against possible Soviet and Vietnamese activity in those waters, Peking's behavior indicates a probable assertiveness in the future that could create problems for the United States and Taiwan as well.

Quasidiplomatic Contacts

Secretary Kissinger's sixth visit to the PRC, and his first as secretary of state, was made in November 1973; it had been somewhat delayed by the outbreak of war in the Middle East. Since the establishment of the liaison offices, no breakthroughs of a diplomatic nature were possible without something resembling American abandonment of Taiwan, something that was out of the question at that time owing to President Nixon's growing political difficulties. The atmosphere was evidently cordial, nevertheless; Kissinger was received by Chairman Mao. The communique spoke optimistically of continuing "normalization" on the basis of the Shanghai Communique; the Chinese side "reiterated that the normalization of relations between China and the United States can be realized only on the basis of confirming the principle of one China," a statement suggesting slightly greater flexibility on the Taiwan question but not really committing Peking to anything (New York Times, 1973a; Washington Post, 1973a).

Regardless of this nuance, or possible nuance, relations between the PRC and the United States were not going well. The staff of the United States Liaison Office in Peking found greater difficulty in getting access to Chinese officials than before. Huang Chen returned to China for several weeks beginning in November 1973, and David Bruce was absent from his post for eight weeks in January-March 1974 (New York Times, 1974e; 1974f). The two main problems appear to have been the upsurge of radical activity in the PRC beginning in the summer of 1973, at the time of the Tenth Party Congress, and Chinese dissatisfaction over the continuation of American relations with the Republic of China (New York Times, 1974d).

It was not until November 11, 1974, after and perhaps on account of the relatively friendly Chinese message of November 6 to the Soviet Union already mentioned, that the announcement of a forthcoming seventh visit by Kissinger to the PRC was issued (New York Times, 1974c). The visit took place at the end of November, following the Ford-Brezhnev summit conference at Vladivostok; Peking had publicly stated some reservations about this choice of a site, since it was on territory that Peking claimed to have been part of China (in reality, the Manchu Empire), but privately Peking indicated that it had no real objection. In any event, the main business of the Kissinger visit, apart from some briefing by the American side on the Vladivostok summit, was a Chinese invitation to President Ford to visit the PRC. Clearly Peking wanted to involve him personally, as President Nixon had involved himself personally, in Sino-American relations and to give Peking an equivalent of the Vladivostok summit, rather than leaving everything to Kissinger. As though to emphasize this point, and perhaps to indicate general dissatisfaction with the state of Sino-American relations, Chairman Mao did not receive Kissinger on this occasion, as he had done twice in 1973 (New York Times, 1974b).

It turned out that there was to be a lapse of almost exactly a year before the Ford visit took place. During this period there were increasingly strong indications of Peking's distress over what it perceived as an American failure, in the name of détente, to cope adequately with the Soviet Union.

The Ford Summit

Secretary Kissinger arrived in Peking on October 19, 1975, for his eighth visit. His main mission was to arrange the details, including the date, for the projected visit by President Ford. He was lectured by the Chinese participants, especially Mao and Vice Premier Teng Hsiao-p'ing (Premier Chou En-lai had been hospitalized since mid-1974), on their discontent with American foreign policy in general, and especially with the allegedly inadequate American handling of the Soviet Union (New York Times, 1975e, 1975f). It is probably significant that no definite date for the Ford visit was announced at that time, very likely because none was agreed on owing to the unpleasant atmosphere surrounding the Kissinger visit. Kissinger himself has been credibly reported to have been so angered by his reception that he recommended that the presidential visit be cut from the projected week to four days (Evans and Novak, 1975).

As it turned out, this was done, and President Ford spent some of his time in Peking working on his budget, as though to signal

American displeasure with the Chinese attitude. The American advance party sent to arrange the administrative details of the Ford visit was delayed in leaving, again apparently on account of the mutual bad feeling (New York Times, 1975c; Washington Post, 1975b).

When the Ford visit finally took place, on December 1-5, 1975, little of substance seems to have been accomplished. A common sense of nonachievement and differences of view was reflected in the absence of a final communique. There were apparently no real negotiations, merely exchanges of views. Mao and Teng lectured Ford, as they had lectured Kissinger, on the shortcomings of American policy, especially policy toward the Soviet Union. The degree of cordiality was little more than was required by the laws of hospitality (Washington Post, 1975a; 1975c; Washington Star, 1975b; New York Times, 1975c; 1975d).

Coolness in Sino-American relations was further suggested by what seemed to be an American effort to downgrade the importance not only of the Ford visit but of the relationship as a whole. On his way home President Ford visited Indonesia and the Philippines, in effect on time saved by reducing the length of the Peking summit. His so-called Pacific Doctrine, announced in Hawaii, reaffirmed the American intention to "normalize" relations with the PRC but the doctrine listed this determination after, and presumably therefore as a lesser priority than an affirmation of the American "partnership" with Japan. The contrast with the days of the "Nixon shocks" of 1971, when the United States clearly found Peking more congenial than Tokyo, was marked, especially since the Pacific Doctrine was proclaimed on December 7, the anniversary of the Japanese attack on Pearl Harbor (New York Times, 1975b).

Another sign, and also an effect, of the cool state of Sino-American relations was the fact that at the time of the Ford visit no replacement for George Bush as head of the United States Liaison Office in Peking was announced; Bush was being called home to become Director of the Central Intelligence Agency. This problem was resolved in March 1976, when President Ford announced his choice of Thomas S. Gates, a senior and respected figure who had been the last secretary of defense under the

Eisenhower administration, to succeed Bush in Peking; Gates was to be given ambassadorial rank, which Bruce and Bush had also held, but of course not formal ambassadorial status because of the absence of full diplomatic relations (Washington Star, 1976).

American Arms For Peking?

Given the PRC's strategic inferiority to the Soviet Union, it would be logical, on practical grounds, for Peking to be interested in buying advanced American conventional weapons and other forms of high technology with military applications. There is some evidence that Chinese proposals along these lines were made as early as 1973 (Pillsbury, 1975: 53).[29] It was reported early in 1974 that the United Aircraft Corporation had received official American permission to sell transport helicopters, in uncertain numbers, to the PRC (New York Times, 1974h; Washington Post, 1974). The following year it was announced that Peking had contracted to buy Spey jet engines—which when married to a suitable airframe such as the PRC can produce, will generate a speed of up to Mach 2.2—from the British Rolls-Royce Company (New York Times, 1975a). The announcement that the United States would resume selling arms to Yugoslavia (Washington Post, 1976b; New York Times, 1976c), another country threatened by possible Soviet military pressures, could not help suggesting the idea of similar sales to the PRC.

There were, however, obvious and serious political and foreign policy obstacles on both sides. It has been plausibly suggested that on the Chinese side the idea of purchasing American arms, as part of the overall program of technological acquisition and economic development, was favored by the moderates including Acting Premer (later Premier) Hua Kuo-feng but was controversial and under attack by the radicals (Zorza, 1976).

There is obviously a great deal of uncertainty on this question, but it seems likely that even if American arms are not actually sold to the PRC the possibility of such sales will be a significant issue on both sides.

7. EFFECTS OF THE SINO-AMERICAN DÉTENTE

After 1969, when Peking emerged from the Cultural Revolution and the Nixon administration took office, changes in both Chinese and American foreign policy beneficial to Sino-American relations were practically inevitable. The PRC was determined to normalize its foreign relations, in order to repair the damage done to them during the Cultural Revolution as well as to cope with the Soviet threat. The United States was determined to withdraw from Vietnam and to minimize the aftereffects of doing so by, among other things, working for a multilateral balance of power in Asia to replace the former Sino-American confrontation. These more or less convergent policies were calculated to produce effects that included not only some form of Sino-American détente but others that might look like results of the détente whether they were or not. In other words, it is difficult to say in some cases whether a particular development in Asian international politics is the outcome specifically of the Sino-American détente or of broader trends of which the new Chinese and American Asian policies were such important features.

With this important reservation in mind, this chapter nevertheless tries to assess the principal effects of the Sino-American détente.

American Behavior Toward Asia

From Peking's point of view, the perspective from which this study mainly tries to approach the subject of Sino-American relations, the most obvious desired effect of the détente was a continued modification of American policy toward the PRC in a direction favorable to Chinese interests. Evidence has been produced to show that by this standard the effects of the Sino-American détente have been mixed, but predominantly favorable.

Until about 1973, Peking appeared to believe that the Sino-American détente was acting as a useful constraint on the Soviet Union, even though the United States denied officially that it perceived its new relationship with the PRC as serving this purpose and insisted that it was maintaining "equidistance" between the two communist adversaries. To be sure, Peking would probably have preferred a more positive stand, such as a declaration by the United States that its détente with the Soviet Union was contingent on Soviet avoidance of an attack on the PRC, or possibly as we have seen a willingness to sell American arms to the PRC. But it was only after 1973, and especially after the Vladivostok summit of 1974, that Peking came to believe strongly that it was not getting its money's worth, so to speak, from the United States as against the Soviet Union. The Chinese reservations related not only to the lack of specific American support for the PRC against the Soviet Union but to the general American policy toward the Soviet Union in such fields as arms control, Europe, and the Third World.

There was a similar negative trend in Peking's evaluation of the American performance with respect to Taiwan, and again the turning point was in 1973-1974. Down to that time Peking apparently believed that the American side not only considered "normalization" to include diplomatic recognition and the cutting of ties with the Republic of China but intended to "normalize" in that sense at the earliest practicable time. After that Peking evidently came to have increasing doubts on this score, in spite of repeated American endorsements of the principle of "normalization." Even if the moderates claimed that the United States had accepted the "principle" of "one China" and that was sufficient for the time being, the radicals apparently disagreed and wanted something more, and their influence was far from negligible.

On the trade and technology front, apart perhaps from arms sales, Peking probably saw more reason to feel satisfied with the American performance. On the other hand, there were problems here too, particularly the heavily adverse balance of trade.

On the American side, it appears that the resignation of President Nixon, the end of the American involvement in Indochina, and the recurrent turmoil in Peking's politics have resulted in a considerable downgrading of the Chinese connection. It seems probable that the two main benefits that the United States still hoped to gain from its détente with Peking were some leverage on the Soviet Union and reasonably good Chinese behavior in Asia. On the second of these scores the results were reasonably good, but they were less impressive on the first; the tie with Peking is only one of several American levers for coping with the Soviet Union, and not necessarily the most useful one, and the effectiveness of all of them taken together has obviously been less than optimal.

On both sides, then, the Sino-American détente has brought some serious disappointments as well as some useful results. Certainly its effect on American behavior toward the PRC has been less marked than Peking could have wished.

Soviet Behavior Toward China

It is of course impossible to say what the probability of a Soviet attack on China would have been in the absence of the Sino-American détente, but whatever the probability it has almost certainly been reduced by the détente. There is reason to believe that at two critical periods in the Sino-Soviet border confrontation of 1969 (March and August-September), Soviet behavior was moderated, not so much by fear of a direct American response as by a fear of driving the PRC into the arms of the United States (Hinton, 1971: 26-27; 29-30). It is also likely that by the second half of 1970 Moscow was aware that there were contacts between the PRC and the United States and was somewhat influenced in its behavior toward the PRC by the knowledge; a possible example is the sending of a Soviet ambassador to Peking in October 1970, for the first time in four years.

The announcement of the first Kissinger visit to Peking was followed by an extraordinary flurry of Soviet diplomatic and propaganda activity obviously designed to cope with the new situation, and by a continued avoidance of a resumption of major direct pressures on the PRC (Hinton, 1971: 4-5).

The last major stage in the development of the Sino-American détente, the establishment of the liaison offices, was probably also the last to make much of an impression on Moscow. After that, the absence of major new developments and the simple passage of time seem to have eroded somewhat the impact of the détente on Soviet thinking (Hinton, 1975c: 26).

Nevertheless, the détente does seem to have exerted a significant constraint on Soviet behavior toward China, although by no means the only such constraint and not necessarily a permanently sufficient one (Hinton, 1975c: 44). Certainly Peking is not relying exclusively on its American connection to restrain Moscow but is also improving its military capabilities and cultivating a broad range of diplomatic relationships. Peking would be doing this in any case, but what it regards as the weakening of the American will to oppose the Soviet Union has made this policy seem all the more necessary. But in spite of its current concern over the American performance, Peking appears to believe that on balance it has gotten some value out of the Sino-American détente as a constraint on Soviet behavior, at least to the point where it is worth continuing the détente for this purpose as well as others.

Soviet Behavior Toward the United States

Soviet behavior toward the United States, as well as toward the PRC, seems to have been significantly affected by the Sino-American détente at least down to about 1973. An example is the Soviet unwillingness to cancel or disrupt the summit conference of May 1972 with President Nixon even on account of the American bombing and mining campaign in Vietnam. The Soviet-American détente, which began at about the same time as the Sino-American détente and proceeded more or less parallel with it, was almost certainly influenced positively by it. In effect, both the two communist adversaries were competitively seeking détente with the United States.

However, the general course of Soviet behavior toward the United States since 1973—the absence of a SALT II agreement, the Soviet adventure in Angola, and so forth—suggests that as problems developed in the Sino-American détente the latter became less effective as an incentive to Moscow to cultivate its own détente with the United States.

Chinese Behavior in Asia

There is little doubt that the Sino-American détente, and in particular the hope of gaining a counterweight to the Soviet Union and of making progress toward the "liberation" of Taiwan, has had a considerable moderating effect on Peking's behavior in Asia. The main influences working in the other direction, Peking's uneasy alliances with Pyongyang and Hanoi, have been more than outweighed by the Chinese determination to refrain, at least for the time being, from overassertiveness in Asia. The desire to maintain the détente with the United States and hasten the American military withdrawal from Taiwan promised in the Shanghai Communique is an important reason, although not the only one. The Sino-American détente, together with such other factors as the Soviet threat, which in turn is a major cause of the détente, has made Peking much more favorably disposed than before toward the American military presence and commitments in the Far East and the Western Pacific including the ties with Japan, which used to be the target of loud denunciations from Peking.

The Sino-American détente is by no means the only source of Peking's recent, relatively moderate, behavior in Asia. Another, probably still more important, is the Sino-Soviet confrontation and Peking's fear that any tension it allowed to develop in its relations with an Asian state would create diplomatic opportunities for the Soviet Union. A similar phenomenon occurred at the beginning of 1960, when an impending visit by Khrushchev to southern Asia appears to have been what led Peking at that time to settle disputes with Burma, Indonesia, and Nepal, and to make an offer of settlement to India (Hinton, 1966: 41). Similarly, Peking has shown an active interest since about 1970 in establishing diplomatic and otherwise "normal" relations with the ASEAN (Association of South East Asia States: Indonesia, Thailand, the Philippines, Malaysia, and Singapore). Its most important motive is probably the Soviet-connected one just mentioned, but it is also possible that Peking is thinking of making a contribution to "diminishing" the "tension in the area" along the lines referred to in the Shanghai Communique.

Asian Accommodation to China

Most students of East Asian international politics would probably agree that the most striking characteristic of recent years has been the tendency of all but a few of the Asian states to seek accommodation with the PRC. This trend got under way in 1968-1969, when it began to become clear that the United States was going to withdraw from Vietnam and would probably reduce its military presence elsewhere in Asia, which had been devoted largely to containing the PRC. To the extent that the American withdrawal was associated with, and in fact presupposed, some form of Sino-American détente, as it did to a significant degree, the process of Asian accommodation to the PRC was indirectly linked to the emergence of the Sino-American détente.

Although Thailand began secret negotiations with the PRC as early as 1968 or 1969, perhaps the first overt sign of the trend came in September 1970, when Malaysian Prime Minister Razak began to propose the "neutralization" of Southeast Asia under the guarantee of the major powers, which he identified as China, the Soviet Union, and the United States, in that order (Hinton, 1976: 151). The general realization after July 1971 that a Sino-

American détente was actually in the making accelerated the trend toward accommodation. The most spectacular result was the recognition of the PRC by Japan in 1972, by Malaysia in 1974, and by the Philippines and Thailand in 1975. The last three wanted, and believed that they got, a degree of assurance from Peking that it would not try to manipulate or incite the overseas Chinese or local revolutionary movements on their soil. Among the ASEAN states, only Indonesia and Singapore stood aloof from this trend, and it appeared likely that eventually they would fall in with it (Rau, 1976: 230-247).

The Asian Balance

With the end of the long war in Indochina in 1975, the Far East appeared on the surface to be closer to peace than it had been for many years. To the extent that this was true, the single main cause was not so much the Sino-American détente as the Sino-Soviet confrontation and Peking's related struggle against the Soviet campaign for a vaguely defined "collective security system" in Asia. The tension between the PRC and the Soviet Union acted much like a boil that drew into itself the toxins from the entire adjacent part of the body. In spite of occasional predictions[30] that the Sino-Soviet dispute would soon come to an end, there was no "hard" evidence to support this prognosis, and most analysts believed, more plausibly, that the dispute would survive at least as long as Mao Tse-tung did. If so, there was no compelling reason to expect a major disruption of the Far Eastern balance as long as the PRC and the Soviet Union continued in their strange current relationship of "neither war nor peace." In that case, the current situation, which is one of a rough quadripolar balance among the PRC, the United States, the Soviet Union, and Japan, appears likely to endure.

8. THE UNITED STATES AS A POLICY PROBLEM FOR PEKING

Clearly Peking's attitudes and policies toward the United States stem from some of the most basic features of its ideology, politics, and foreign policy. These need a rather more systematic discussion than they have been given so far, as an aid to evaluating the future of the Sino-American relationship.

Chinese Politics and the United States

There is little doubt that the radicals in Peking, with the partial exception of Mao Tse-tung himself, have had strong reservations about the Sino-American détente and have been the main obstacle to it on the Chinese side. Their objections are ideologically based to a considerable extent: to them, the United States is the leading "imperialist" state, an oppressive "superpower" like the Soviet Union. They appear to be more emotionally involved than their moderate colleagues in the Taiwan question and the obstacles that the United States poses to the island's "liberation." Their relatively defiant attitude toward Soviet "social-imperialism" suggests that they are less impressed than the moderates with the need for the détente with the United States as a constraint on the Soviet Union. Even though they have accepted the need for some form of improved government-to-government relations with the United States, they insist on the importance of an aggressive "people's diplomacy" aimed at influencing American public opinion not only in the direction of a more favorable image of the PRC but also, at least in theory, in the direction of an ultimate revolution in the United States.

It is therefore not surprising that the state of Sino-American relations has borne a rough inverse relationship to the political influence of the radicals. After the fall of Lin Piao, who had been the most powerful of them apart from Chairman Mao himself, in September 1971, the radicals were on the defensive for about two years, and it was almost certainly not a coincidence that those years saw the high point of the Sino-American relationship to date.

In early August 1973, however, the radicals began to reassert themselves, the initial overt indication of this tendency being a propaganda campaign against Confucius, whom one would have thought to have been dead for some time but who in this connection appeared to symbolize Chou En-lai. This radical resurgence was evoked partly by the approach of the Tenth Party Congress, which was held later in August. Another likely consideration was that exactly seven years before, in early August 1966, Mao had said that China needed a "great upheaval" every seven or eight years. The moderates under Chou En-lai counterattacked after early 1974 by linking the relatively new campaign against Confucius with the older campaign against the defunct Lin Piao, by stressing the need for unity and order for the sake of the economy, and the like. The moderates both reasserted and endangered their influence over the regional military, whose strong political position in the provinces had been a major problem since 1967, by beginning in mid-1973 to deemphasize (for devious political reasons) the Soviet threat to China—which previously had been emphasized partly in order to enhance the loyalty of the regional military to the center—and by ramming through a series of transfers of the major military region commanders in December 1973. The latter move evidently created some resentment among the senior military, which was to show itself, especially after the death of Chou En-lai in January 1976, in the form of a partial revival of the alliance of the early and mid-1960s between the radicals and some of the more politically inclined members of the military leadership. It should be understood that the moderates continued, even after the death of Chou, to hold most of the high political ground, including the Foreign Ministry, but they were generally on the defensive, both psychologically and in the important field of propaganda.

One of the areas in which the moderates could do no more than hold the line after 1973 was that of policy toward the United States; this was true not only because of political developments in China, but because of the hesitation on the American side about moving ahead with "normalization." Officials of the United States Liaison Office in Peking found their contacts with the Foreign Ministry more restricted than before. Visas for Americans wanting to visit the PRC were handed out somewhat more sparingly than before. The appointment in mid-1974 of Wang Hai-jung, who was generally believed to be Mao Tse-tung's niece, as director of the Foreign Ministry's division concerned with American affairs seemed to put the highest possible stamp of approval on the Sino-American relationship, but it also suggested that the chairman himself was monitoring that relationship with special care and would not permit it to deviate from what he considered proper.

A number of trends and incidents in the field of Sino-American cultural relations during this period indicated both the continuing and evidently growing influence of the radicals and their touchiness on matters of "principle," as they called it. To an even greater extent than the Soviet Union, the PRC insisted on controlling the selection, itineraries, and agendas not only of its own citizens visiting the United States but of American citizens going the other way (Cohen, 1974). The PRC insisted on the barring of newsmen from the Republic of China, the Republic of Korea, South Africa, and Israel from the preview of an archaeological exhibit from the PRC in Washington and thereby brought on the cancellation of the preview, although not of the exhibit itself (New York Times, 1974a). The PRC cancelled an American tour of a Chinese entertainment troupe rather than agree to an

American request that it drop from its program a song about the "liberation" of Taiwan (Washington Post, 1975e). A delegation of American mayors cancelled a visit to the PRC because the Chinese refused to allow the mayor of San Juan to accompany the group, Puerto Rico evidently being regarded by Peking as a colony (Washington Post, 1975d). The arrival in the United States of a dance troupe of Tibetan exiles brought on a strong protest by the Chinese Foreign Ministry to the effect that the United States was interfering in China's internal affairs and committing a "flagrant violation" of the Shanghai Communique (New York Times, 1975g). One of the probable reasons for the radicals' sensitivity was the fact that in 1972-1973 Chiang Ch'ing herself had been involved for some reason in sponsoring cultural contacts with the West, such as visits by the Italian film maker Antonioni and the Philadelphia Symphony Orchestra, and that in early 1974 a brief but intense propaganda campaign had been launched against these and other manifestations of Western culture, at whose initiative is not clear. After that the radicals evidently felt compelled to behave with their usual militant orthodoxy in such matters.

These trends and events made it virtually certain that as long as the radicals remained an influential force in Chinese politics, or in other words at least for the remainder of Chairman Mao's life, similar problems would continue to complicate the Sino-American relationship from the Chinese side. Whether after that the PRC would cease to have an adversary-requiring political system, and whether or not its list of adversaries would still include the United States, remained to be seen.

The Chinese View of American Politics

Although it has been trying hard to learn, Peking evidently does not yet understand the American political process very well. In this respect it compares unfavorably with the Soviet Union, one reason for the difference being the obvious fact that Moscow has maintained an embassy in Washington for 40 years longer than the PRC has had its Liaison Office there. Even though

Peking has apparently outgrown the crudest of its Marxist stereo-
types about the United States in its thinking, although not in its
propaganda, it still tends to overestimate the elitist elements in
American politics and to underestimate the importance of public
opinion.

The first American president for whom Peking felt any real
approval was of course Nixon, and this was because of his China
policy and his seemingly tough line toward the Soviet Union.
Since it approved of him, it had difficulty in understanding why a
growing percentage of the American public did not and why there
was so much uproar over the Watergate "bugging" and the ensuing "coverup." There is evidently rather little "bugging" in
Peking for one reason or another, in sharp contrast to Moscow;
and even if there were, it would never be allowed to develop into
a major political issue. The main effect on Peking of the Watergate crisis and President Nixon's resignation, as well the growing
foreign policy role of Congress during the same period, was to
shake its confidence in the political stability and reliability of the
U.S. as a foreign policy partner. This reaction was of course not
unique to Peking.

In the PRC as elsewhere, President Ford was initially a virtual
unknown quantity. Peking shortly, and correctly, seems to have
come to see him as guided by Secretary Kissinger in foreign
policy matters to a greater extent than Nixon had been. As
already suggested, Kissinger himself appeared to Peking as excessively committed to the Soviet-American détente and prone to
give it priority over the Sino-American relationship. By contrast,
Peking liked Secretary of Defense James R. Schlesinger for his
relatively hardnosed attitude toward the Soviet Union [31] and was
clearly distressed when he was purged in the so-called Sunday
Night Massacre (November 2, 1975). There were reports that
Peking had been planning to invite him for a visit.

Peking's hopes for the 1976 election seem to center on Gover-
nor Reagan and Senator Jackson, both of whom took an anti-
Soviet line and neither of whom would be likely to reappoint
Kissinger as Secretary of State. The Democratic hopefuls to the
left of Jackson are generally suspect in Peking's eyes as soft on
the Soviet Union.

The Taiwan Issue

It is possible that the radicals in Peking believe that if the United States were to cut its ties with Taiwan and establish diplomatic relations with the PRC, the Republic of China would feel compelled to reach an accommodation with the mainland. If so, this would help to account for the apparently greater eagerness of the radicals, as compared with the moderates, to press the United States to withdraw from Taiwan as soon as possible. The moderates, for their part, almost certainly realize that the Republic of China might well survive a cutting of its ties with the United States and retain a formidable economic and military capability, or in other words that a termination of the American commitment to Taiwan would not necessarily lead promptly to the "liberation" of Taiwan and the end of the long Chinese civil war.

Regardless of the future of the American commitment to Taiwan, its past history (since 1950) is so imposing that its termination might have serious effects in other quarters beside Taiwan itself. The paradox is that, even though Peking wants the United States to terminate its commitment, the United States would probably not gain increased respect from either the radicals or the moderates, but rather the reverse, by actually terminating it. The United States would enhance the impression it has already made on Peking by its behavior elsewhere, especially in Asia, of a power whose commitments are less dependable than they ought to be.

The American Role in Asia

Since the defeat of Japan, the three main acts of American involvement in Asia have been aimed at coping successively with North Korea, the PRC, and North Vietnam. Of these the last is now over, the second has been greatly modified, and the first is being called somewhat into question through the gradual reduction of the American military presence in South Korea.

Although Peking has benefited from this process on the whole, it has felt for the past few years, as already indicated, that the United States has done about enough in disengaging itself militarily from Asia and the Western Pacific and that further withdrawals might create opportunities for the Soviet Union.

By roughly the same logic, Peking was apparently not only surprised but dismayed by the suddenness and completeness of Hanoi's victory in South Vietnam in the spring of 1975, for two main reasons. In the first place, the victory threatened to make Hanoi an even more formidable rival of Peking for influence in Southeast Asia. Secondly, the ultimate failure of the long American effort to prevent a communist takeover of South Vietnam reflected badly on the effectiveness of the United States as an Asian power.

There were other things as well about the American performance in Asia that Peking evidently found unsatisfactory, or at least insufficiently dependable. In Korea, where Peking's main desire is for stability, the United States by its tendency to withdraw is threatening that stability. As for Japan, Peking is anxious that it not rearm massively, especially with nuclear weapons, or move closer to the Soviet Union, and either or both of these could be the result of the current image of indecisiveness that the United States projects about its future military role in Asia, including its commitment to Japan. The Indonesian military, which has an obsession with the idea of a possible upsurge of Chinese-supported communist insurgency and is essentially hostile to the PRC, is approaching the United States for arms, and Peking presumably hopes that they will not be forthcoming. Peking probably hopes that the United States will restrain its hostility to the new regime in Cambodia and will look with favor on its closeness to the PRC and even Thailand as a constraint on possible Vietnamese pressures. Peking would undoubtedly like the United States to do more for Pakistan and Bangla Desh, both of which consider themselves threatened by India; at present Pakistan, although a fairly close ally of the United States until recently, receives most of its external support from the PRC and Iran.

The Soviet Problem

Peking, radicals and moderates alike, perceives the Soviet Union as aiming at "hegemony" in Asia and indeed the world. Peking remembers and appears to regard as significant the fact that the United States expressed itself in the Shanghai Communique as "opposed to efforts by any other country or group of countries to establish such hegemony" in the "Asia-Pacific region." In spite of occasional propaganda statements to the contrary, Peking no longer regards the United States as bent on "hegemony," at least in Asia; the problem is of course the Soviet Union, in Peking's opinion at any rate. This message has been hammered on by Chinese leaders in numerous conversations with Americans, official and unofficial, and they have made it clear that in their opinion the United States is not doing enough to combat the alleged Soviet drive for "hegemony" at either the Asian or the global level. The problem is made all the more painful in Chinese eyes by the memory of the considerable political effort that Peking has invested in its American connection in the hope that the United States would cooperate effectively with it in opposing Soviet efforts to establish "hegemony." One of the few cards Peking has to play if it is to get the United States to do better in this respect is to suggest that if the United States does not do better Peking itself may seek an accommodation with the Soviet Union; this may have been one of the messages that Peking intended to convey when on December 27, 1975, it released the three Soviet helicopter crewmen whom it had taken prisoner in March 1974.

9. POSSIBLE FUTURE PROBLEMS FOR
SINO-AMERICAN DÉTENTE

S ince the Sino-American relationship down to the mid- or late 1960s was essentially an adversary one, it was inevitable that the Sino-American détente of the early 1970s should be complicated by the existence of serious problems. These have been discussed in previous chapters. The existence of these problems makes it practically certain that there will also be problems in the future, probably of a similar nature but not necessarily identical. Because of the shortcomings of the analytical methods employed and the predictable occurrence of unpredictable events, any forecast of these future problems is bound to be seriously in error. The best that can be done is to suggest the areas in which the problems might arise and the general shape that they might take.

Mutual Disillusionment

Perhaps the most obvious category of possible problems is what could be called mutual disillusionment. For each side, even the current incomplete Sino-American relationship represents a considerable shift from previous policy, and the question inevitably arises whether it has been worth the political cost and effort. On the Chinese side, there has apparently been some feeling that the point of diminishing, or even zero, returns may have been reached with respect to the three main purposes for which Peking appears to have entered into its new relationship with the United States. In other words, it could be held that the PRC has not gotten sufficient value from the United States as a constraint on possible Soviet behavior toward China, that the United States has not only been unable so far but may never make up its mind to break with the Republic of China and "normalize" relations with the PRC, and that China cannot afford American technology on a large scale and in any case would be politically corrupted by it. There are also other, less important respects in which from Peking's perspective the Sino-American relationship might appear not to have come up to expectations. On the American side, the argument could be made that the PRC remains essentially an adversary and even a threat, that therefore no concessions to it are justifiable except to the extent that they clearly serve American interests, and that now that the United States is no longer involved significantly in Indochina no further need for concessions to the PRC exists.

Arguments of this general nature are likely to be heard on both sides in the future, even if the interests of the two sides never come into direct conflict with each other. It is quite possible that such arguments could carry enough weight on one side or the other—it would not have to be on both sides—to prevent any further significant development of the Sino-American détente. But to undo what has already been achieved, or in other words to revert to something like the earlier fullblown adversary relationship, some major overt hostile act on one side or the other would probably be required. That is also conceivable, even though not very likely at present.

Political Pitfalls

Earlier chapters have established a strong probability that the Maoist radicals in Peking are basically opposed to the Sino-

American détente on ideological and emotional grounds, and that they will continue to be a significant force in Chinese politics for some time to come. Their resurgence since 1973 and their success in blocking the expected succession of Teng Hsiao-p'ing to Chou En-lai as premier suggest that their influence may grow still greater in the future, or at least for certain periods. If that happens, it could very well spell trouble for the Sino-American détente. It could lead, for example, to greater pushiness on the Taiwan question, or in other words to a demand that the United States proceed immediately to break with the Republic of China and "normalize" relations with the PRC, under penalty of the closing down of the liaison offices.

On the American side, the objections and threat to the Sino-American relationship come not from the left but from the right. A recent Gallup Poll indicated that 70 percent of the public is unwilling to see American recognition withdrawn from the Republic of China even if that is necessary to the establishment of diplomatic relations with the PRC (Gallup Organization, 1975). The conservative sector of American public opinion clearly feels a continuing sense of obligation to the Republic of China and probably sees trade as the main concrete benefit of the détente with the PRC. Like the radicals in China, the conservatives in the United States are obviously going to remain a significant, although not necessarily dominant, political force, but they are less likely to take or demand action directly calculated to complicate the Sino-American détente.

Tension Over Korea

Apart from the Sino-Soviet border, Korea is probably the most explosive area in Asia. The seeming détente between the two Koreas after 1972 has practically collapsed. Each side is heavily armed, politically tense, and experiencing difficulties with both its domestic economy and its international balance of payments. The North is allied with the Soviet Union and the South (the PRC) with the United States. Fortunately, there is a considerable degree of mutual deterrence between the two sides, and the allies of each try to restrain it while promising to protect it. One indication of the interest in Korean stability on Peking's part is the fact that for several years no reference to the Sino-North Korean alliance has appeared in the Chinese press, even on occasions when mention would have been appropriate.

If, in spite of the wishes of the other powers, war should break out between the two Koreas, a serious strain would be imposed on the Sino-American détente. The PRC would probably feel obligated to declare support for North Korea and perhaps to send it some arms. The United States would be somewhat more heavily involved on the side of South Korea, especially if American troops were still stationed there. As in the case of the Vietnam war, the PRC and the United States would probably work out some way, by means of both direct contacts and indirect signals, to minimize the likelihood of another Sino-American war similar to the one of 1950-1953. But the danger of a serious disruption of the Sino-American détente would still exist, even if no Sino-American war broke out. For this reason, as well as for many others, the outbreak of another conflict in the Korean peninsula is an eventuality to be avoided by all useful means.

The China Sea

Because of its suspected oil reserves and its naval and commercial importance, the China Sea is likely to be a significant arena of interaction among a number of major powers and regional states, the PRC and the United States in particular. The PRC clearly regards its continental shelf, including Taiwan and the South China Sea, as part of its rightful sphere of influence and intends to become increasingly assertive there. Chinese naval activity in the South China Sea has shown a sharp increase (New York Times, 1976b). Assuming that the China Sea does contain major oil deposits, Japan is bound to feel a keen interest in them. It is not hard to imagine a prolonged, complex, triangular interaction among Chinese claims supported by naval activity, American oil companies, and Japanese demand for oil. Depending on a number of imponderables more political than economic in nature, the result could be the promotion of either cooperation or hostility between any two of the three, or among all three. This is not a very helpful statement, but none that is much more helpful is possible on the basis of the evidence now available.

Peking's Nuclear Progress

The exact level of the PRC's strategic forces (that is, nuclear warheads and appropriate delivery systems) at any given time is known only approximately outside China and in any case is less important than the fact that Peking is generally known to be making steady, although not very spectacular, progress toward the status of a major nuclear power. [32] Its presumed objective is to acquire as soon as possible a dependable second-strike deterrent against its potential nuclear adversaries, meaning mainly the Soviet Union but also, at least in theory, the United States. Deterrence is a state of mind existing solely in the mind of the deterred, and it is therefore impossible for any one else, including the adversary who is trying to exercise deterrence, to predict with certainty what level of retaliatory capability will create a state of deterrence. Subject to this uncertainty, it appears that the PRC may already possess a minimum deterrent against the Soviet Union, on which it has evidently targeted most of its operational missiles. Since the PRC has as yet no comparable capability to deliver nuclear or thermonuclear warheads, by missile or otherwise, against the continental United States, there is no reliable Chinese deterrent against the United States. The PRC can probably deliver a retaliatory nuclear attack against at least some of the forces, bases, and allies of the United States in the Far East, but it is doubtful whether that capability constitutes a "credible" deterrent; for one thing, the political cost to the PRC of visiting nuclear devastation on another Asian country, even in retaliation for an American nuclear threat or actual attack on the PRC, would be enormous.

On the other hand, even if the growth of the PRC's nuclear capability does not create any necessary grounds for alarm with respect to the future of the Sino-American détente, neither does it afford a basis for complacency. An eminent authority on Chinese foreign policy has pointed out that the belief on Peking's part that it possesses an effective second-strike capability may make it more assertive in responding to threats, real or imagined, to its security (Whiting, 1975: 226, 243). It is of course conceivable, although less likely, that under cover of its second-strike capability the PRC might grow genuinely aggressive in Asia, as it has not been to date; there are important political and military costs and risks attached to such a course of action, but it cannot be ruled out.

There is an obvious attractiveness to the idea of trying to involve the PRC in some sort of arms control or disarmament arrangements (Clough et al., 1975). The problem is that, since the PRC considers such arrangements to be of the nature of "principle" and since they are politically controversial in Peking, the PRC has so far refused to enter into any, except for a no-first-use agreement among the nuclear powers, and shows no signs of changing its mind to any significant extent. The idea of entering into a no-first-use agreement with the PRC, even though Peking has often said that even without such an agreement it would never be the first to use nuclear weapons, presents serious problems for the United States, mainly because such an agreement would wipe out the American capability to deter possible Chinese conventional aggression by nuclear means, and so far it has not been formally accepted by the American side. Arms control does not appear to be one of the most promising fields of Sino-American interaction, at least in the near future.

Chinese Assertiveness in Asia

Even if the nuclear problem is ignored, there is a possibility that the PRC may become assertive in Asia to the point where, consciously or unconsciously, it endangers the Sino-American détente. It is not very likely that such a tendency, if it occurs, will take the form of overt military aggression or attempts at outright political domination (Taylor, 1974: 375-376).

What then is the problem, or possible problem? It is that the PRC may try successfully to enhance its influence by methods and to an extent that create serious difficulties for the other major powers, including the United States, and for one or more of the regional states. The most obvious, and probably the most serious, possibility of this kind is increased Chinese support for leftist and/or tribal insurgency in Southeast Asia. To date, with the complex exception of the fortunately unique situation in Indochina, the PRC has generally and consciously refrained from involving itself in activity of this kind at a level that would threaten to produce a serious crisis in its relations with one of the other major powers or with one of the regional states. Unless a dramatic weakening of one or more of these states offers Peking unexpectedly tempting opportunities, there is only one discernible factor that might lead the PRC to escalate to such a level. That is competition—so far more potential than actual—from Hanoi for revolutionary leadership in the region through the supplying of arms and advice to insurgent movements. There are some recent signs that Hanoi, with its self-confidence enhanced through victory, and with a huge stockpile of American as well as Soviet weapons, may intend to increase its involvement along these lines, perhaps in conscious competition with the PRC. If so, Peking will probably feel compelled to increase its own involvement in support of insurgency in selected areas, Burma and Thailand being obvious possibilities. Such a trend, if it materializes, could very well impose some serious strains on the Sino-American détente, unless the United States decides simply to write off Southeast Asia as an arena of political and strategic interest.

A Sino-Soviet Rapprochement

Short of a Sino-American war, which seems unlikely, the eventuality that would create the greatest strain on the Sino-American détente would probably be a rapprochement between the PRC and the Soviet Union.

As already suggested, this seems unlikely, or at any rate there is no convincing evidence that rapprochement is in prospect and there are an abundance of obstacles to one. On the other hand, there are some powerful reasons why such a development would be in the interest of both parties, one being that it would tend to increase their leverage on the United States and on countries friendly to it. On the other hand, a Sino-Soviet rapprochement need not be seriously adverse to American interests in the long run, especially since even if it occurred it would probably not go as far as a restoration of the rather close working relationship of the early 1950s. But in the short run, a trend toward a Sino-Soviet rapprochement would be very disturbing to the United States; this is probably a major reason why each party occasionally suggests, contrary to the weight of the evidence, that such a rapprochement may be in the making. Since one of the main American motives in seeking détente with the PRC was to gain increased leverage on the Soviet Union, and since the PRC at that time gave the United States every reason to believe it was sincere in saying (as it did in a statement of October 7, 1969) that there were "irreconcilable differences of principle" between it and the Soviet Union, the United States would be justified in considering a rapprochement with the Soviet Union on Peking's part to be, at the minimum, a grave violation of the Shanghai Communique and of Peking's own pledge to maintain its opposition to Soviet efforts at "hegemony."

10. CONCLUSION: AN IRREVERSIBLE DÉTENTE?

The question implied in the title of this chapter is easily answered: there is no such thing as an irreversible political relationship. The current Soviet-American détente, however, has been called irreversible on both sides, officially, and at the highest levels. Secretary Kissinger has come fairly close to doing the same in the case of the Sino-American détente by assuring Peking that "no matter what happens in the United States, friendship with the People's Republic of China is one of the constant factors of American foreign policy" (quoted in The Washington Post, 1973b). However intended, this kind of talk from such a source suggests a need for further discussion of the subject.

It is a doubtful service even to the atmospherics of the Sino-American relationship to make statements as obviously unfounded as this. No one can say how future political leadership on either side will view that relationship. Enough possible problems were indicated in the preceding chapter to show the folly of any talk about the "irreversibility" of the Sino-American détente.

If that is so, does it follow that the United States should cultivate the détente more industriously, or in other words make further concessions to the PRC in the name of détente? Not necessarily, and in fact probably not. From the long term perspective, the United States has probably already made too many concessions too soon to Peking, for too slight a tangible return. Perhaps the main single long range effect of these concessions has been to diminish the respect in which the United States is held in Asia and even in Peking itself. These concessions, especially those at the expense of the Republic of China, have been made not only in the hope of a tangible return—which has not been forth-coming to any great extent except perhaps in the form of the recent absence of serious Chinese troublemaking in Asia—but in the belief that the United States owed the PRC compensation for past wrongs. This belief is highly debatable as a matter of fact; the PRC made its own contribution, and a substantial one, to the origins and course of Sino-American hostility. In any case, no great power can afford, or should be expected, to make its policy on any such basis. In spite of the concessions it has made and the setbacks it has sustained, the United States is not, or at least not yet, a second class power, and it ought not to behave like one.

The soundest, and in fact the only sound, basis for American policy toward the PRC and the Sino-American détente in the future is one of strict reciprocity, or what Peking itself likes to call equality and mutual benefit. The realization of this principle would require Peking to take a less tactical and instrumental view of the Sino-American relationship and to moderate its ideological and political hostility to the United States, both in its propaganda and in its thinking. Only when Peking matures to this point will a true and fruitful détente with it become a reality.

NOTES

1. These sympathies and private contacts in the pre-1949 period are surveyed in Shewmaker (1971).

2. This argument, and similar ones, are developed in Service (1971: esp. 167ff.); U.S. Government (1972: 194-195); and Tuchman (1972).

3. For a trenchant analysis and criticism of these attitudes by a former admirer, see Lindsay (1955).

4. These favorable references to the United States have been deleted from the post-1949 versions.

5. Earlier the Department of State had actively considered diplomatic recognition of Peking (see evidence cited by Harold C. Hinton in U.S. Department of State, 1966: 388).

6. Text broadcast by New China News Agency, November 23, 1949. For a fuller discussion of this subject, see Hinton (1966:68ff.).

7. See the celebrated speech of January 12, 1950 by Secretary Acheson at the National Press Club (1950: 114-115).

8. The best general book on the Korean War is Rees (1964). An interesting recent revisionist interpretation is Simmons (1975).

9. The standard work on Chinese intervention in the Korean War is Whiting (1960).

10. The standard work on the Geneva Conference is Randle (1969).

11. The standard work on the early years of the Sino-Soviet dispute is Zagoria (1962).

12. The best treatment of this period in the Sino-Soviet dispute is Griffith (1964).

13. See the 1966 hearings cited in U.S. Government (1966).

14. For example, Soviet officials began to make contact with American China-watchers in 1966 to learn whether in fact Sino-American "collusion" was in the making.

15. For an excellent analysis of the Nixon Doctrine differing somewhat from this one, see Simon (1975: 6-11).

16. Text released by New China News Agency, May 20, 1970.

17. Personal information.

18. This point was made openly, although rather esoterically, through the republication on August 17, 1971, of a work of 1940 by Mao Tse-tung, "On Policy," in which he defended the policy of collaborating with some lesser adversaries, including foreign countries such as the United States, against the Japanese.

19. Huang's statement of June 1970 cited in Taylor (1974:159); and Huang's 1971 Army Day Speech, text released by New China News Agency (July 31, 1971).

20. Personal information.

21. Except where otherwise indicated, this chapter is based on the general coverage of the Nixon visit in the Western press, especially The

New York Times; on Kalb and Kalb (1974); and of course on the author's own analysis.

22. Soviet sources have charged privately that Peking encouraged the Easter Offensive in order to disrupt the Moscow summit; see Kraft (1972).

23. Personal information.

24. Text of joint communique and Kissinger press conference in New York Times (1973d); also Washington Post (1973c).

25. Personal information.

26. Personal information.

27. Remarks of Senator Mike Mansfield (1974).

28. For general information on the PRC's oil industry see Williams (1975:225-263); and Cheng (1976).

29. Personal information available to the author confirms that the PRC has made private approaches to some of the American firms producing advanced conventional weapons systems. On the tentative approach of the U.S. government to this question, see Washington Post (1976a).

30. For example, by Victor Zorza in several columns in the Washington Post.

31. For a statement of Schlesinger's views after his forced resignation, see his article (1976).

32. For a good discussion of the PRC's nuclear capability, see Fraser (1973: 13-16).

REFERENCES

ACHESON, D. (1951) Statement of January 10, 1950, quoted in Nomination of Philip C. Jessup. Washington: U.S. Gov. Printing Office.

——— (1950) Speech of January 12, 1950 at the National Press Club, quoted in Dept. of State Bulletin (January 23): 114-115.

BELOFF, M. (1953) Soviet Policy in the Far East, 1944-1951. Oxford: Oxford Univ. Press.

BRANDON, H. (1972) The Retreat of American Power. New York: Doubleday.

CHENG Chu-yuan (1976) China's Petroleum Industry: Output Growth and Export Potential. New York: Praeger.

CHOU En-lai (1949) Speech of January 10, 1947, pp. 706-710 in United States Relations with China, with Special Reference to the Period 1944-1949 (the White Paper). Washington: U.S. Dept. of State.

Christian Science Monitor (1972) July 5.

CLARK, W. and M. AVERY (1975) "The Sino-American commercial relationship." in China: A Reassessment of the Economy. Washington: U.S. Gov. Printing Office.

CLOUGH, R. N. et al. (1975) The United States, China, and Arms Control. Washington: Brookings Institution.

COHEN, J. A. (1974) "U.S.-China relations." New York Times (December 18).

Committee of Concerned Asian Scholars (1972) China: Inside the People's Republic. New York: Bantam.

DULLES, F. R. (1972) American Policy Toward Communist China: The Historical Record, 1949-1969. New York: Crowell.

ECKSTEIN, A. (1975) "China's trade policy and Sino-American relations." Foreign Affairs 54, 1 (October).

EVANS, R. and R. NOVAK (1975) Column in Washington Post (December 1).

––– (1972) Column in Washington Post (March 1).

FRASER, A. (1973) The People's Liberation Army: Communist China's Armed Forces. New York: Crane, Russak.

Gallup Organization (1975) A Gallup Study of Public Attitudes Toward Nations of the World, October 1975. Princeton, New Jersey: Gallup.

GRIFFITH, W. E. (1964) The Sino-Soviet Rift. Cambridge: MIT Press.

GURTOV, M. (1967) The First Vietnam Crisis. New York: Columbia Univ. Press.

HARRISON, S. (1975) "Time Bomb in East Asia." Foreign Policy 20 (Fall): 3-27.

HENRY, E. [pseudonym] (1974) "What do the men in the Chungnanhai Palace want?" Far Eastern Affairs 1:129-139 (Moscow).

HINTON, H. C. (1976) "The Soviet campaign for collective security in Asia." Pacific Community 7,2 (January).

––– (1975a) Three and a Half Powers: the New Balance in Asia. Indiana Univ. Press.

––– (1975b) "Implications for the People's Republic of China of an American military withdrawal from Korea." pp. 25-51 in The Maintenance of U.S. Forces in Korea. Strategic Studies Center, Stanford Research Institute.

––– (1975c) "The United States and the Sino-Soviet confrontation." Orbix xix, 1 (Spring).

––– (1974) "East Asia." pp. 124-125 in K. L. London (ed.) The Soviet Impact on World Politics. New York: Hawthorn.

––– (1973a) China's Turbulent Quest: An Analysis of China's Foreign Relations since 1945 (rev. ed.). Indiana Univ. Press.

––– (1973b) "Chinese policy toward Korea." pp. 15-27 in Y. Kim (ed.) Major Powers and Korea. Silver Spring, Md.: Research Institute on Korean Affairs.

––– (1971) The Bear at the Gate: Chinese Policymaking under Soviet Pressure. Washington: American Enterprise Institute and Stanford: Hoover Institution.

––– (1968) "China and Vietnam." pp. 201-224 in Tang Tsou (ed.) China's Policies in Asia and America's Alternatives. Chicago: Univ. of Chicago Press.

94

––– (1966) Communist China in World Politics. Boston: Houghton Mifflin.

Institute of International Relations (1974) Chinese Communist Document: Outline of Education on Situation for Companies. Taipei: Institute of Internatl. Relations (June).

KALB, B. and M. KALB (1974) Kissinger. Boston: Little, Brown.

KOH, B. C. (1976) "The battle without victors: the Korean question in the 30th Session of the U.N. General Assembly." J. of Korean Affairs v, 4 (January): 43-63.

KRAFT, J. (1972) Column in Washington Post (May 25).

KUN, J. C. [j.c.k.] (1972) "Sino-Soviet agreement on Vietnam supplies reported." Radio Free Europe Research Papers (September).

LI, V. H. (1975) "China and off-shore oil: the Tiao-yü-t'ai dispute." pp. 143-162 in B. Garth (ed.) China's Changing Role in the World Economy. New York: Praeger.

LIN Piao (1965) Long Live the Victory of People's War. Peking: Foreign Language Press.

LINDSAY, M. (1955) China and the Cold War: A Study in International Politics. Melbourne Univ. Press.

LIU Shao-ch'i (1951) On Internationalism and Nationalism. Peking: Foreign Language Press.

LU Ting-yi (1951) "The world significance of the Chinese revolution." People's China (July 1).

––– (1949) "Memorandum." pp. 710-719 in United States Relations with China, with Special Reference to the Period 1944-1949 (the White Paper). Washington: U.S. Dept. of State.

LUTHER, D. G. (1975) "China, lump settlements, and executive agreements." pp. 213-222 in B. Garth (ed.) China's Changing Role in the World Economy. New York: Praeger.

MANSFIELD, M. (1974) Remarks, reported in Washington Post (December 15).

MAO Tse-tung (1967) "On the people's democratic dictatorship." (June 30, 1949) pp. 302-315 in Selected Readings from the Works of Mao Tse-tung. Peking: Foreign Languages Press.

––– (1961) Selected Works of Mao Tse-tung Vol. 4. Peking: Foreign Languages Press.

––– (1948) Mao Tse-tung hsuan-chi. Northeast Pub. House. Translated in S. Gelder, The Chinese Communists (pp. 1-60). London: Gollancz (1946).

New York Times (1976a) March 6.
––– (1976b) January 25.
––– (1976c) January 14.
––– (1975a) December 15.
––– (1975b) December 8.
––– (1975c) December 5.
––– (1975d) December 4.
––– (1975e) October 20.
––– (1975f) October 15.
––– (1975g) January 28.
––– (1974a) December 11.
––– (1974h) January 16.
––– (1974b) December 2.
––– (1974c) November 12.
––– (1974d) September 5.
––– (1974e) March 23.
––– (1974f) February 26.
––– (1974g) January 21.
––– (1973a) November 15.
––– (1973b) February 26.
––– (1973c) February 25.
––– (1973d) February 23.

——— (1973e) January 31.

——— (1972a) December 29.

——— (1972b) September 15.

——— (1972c) May 26.

——— (1972d) May 20.

——— (1972e) May 12.

——— (1972f) March 10.

——— (1971) July 10.

——— (1970) The New York Times Report from Red China. New York: Avon.

——— (1967) January 17.

North Shensi Radio (1948) "Congratulations on the opening of the Southeast Asia Youth Conference." North Shensi Radio broadcast (February 16).

PARK, Choon-ho (1975) "The Sino-Japanese-Korean sea resources controversy and the hypothesis of a 200-mile economic zone." Harvard Internatl. Law J. 16, 1 (Winter): 27-46.

——— (1973) "Oil under troubled waters: the Northeast Asia sea-bed controversy." Harvard Internatl. Law J. 14, 2 (Spring): 212-260.

PARK, C. and J. A. COHEN (1975) "The politics of China's oil weapon." Foreign Policy 20 (Fall): 28-49.

PILLSBURY, M. (1975) "U.S.-Chinese military ties?" Foreign Policy 20 (Fall): 53.

RANDLE, R. F. (1969) Geneva 1954: The Indochina War. Princeton: Princeton Univ. Press.

RAU, R. L. (1976) "Normalization with PRC: with emphasis on ASEAN states." Pacific Community 7, 2 (January): 230-247.

REES, D. (1964) Korea: The Limited War. New York: St. Martin's Press.

RESTON, J. (1971) Interview with Chou En-lai in the New York Times (August 10).

SALISBURY, H. (1972) Article in the New York Times (May 12).

SCHLESINGER, J. (1976) "A testing time for America." Fortune xciii, 2 (February): 74-77, 147-149, 153.

SERVICE, J. S. (1971) The Amerasia Papers: Some Problems in the History of U.S.-China Relations. Berkeley, California: Center for Chinese Studies, Univ. of California.

SHEWMAKER, K. E. (1971) Americans and Chinese Communists, 1927-1945: A Persuading Encounter. Ithaca, N.Y.: Cornell Univ. Press.

SHINKICHI (1972) "Japan and China—a new stage?" Problems of Communism xxi, 6 (November-December): 4.

SIMMONS, R. R. (1975) The Strained Alliance: Peking, Pyongyang, Moscow and the Politics of the Korean Civil War. New York: Free Press.

SIMON, S. W. (1975) Asian Neutralism and U.S. Policy. Washington: American Enterprise Institute.

SNOW, E. (1971a) The Long Revolution. New York: Random House.

——— (1971b) "A conversation with Mao Tse-tung." Life (April 30).

TANG Tsou (1963) America's Failure in China, 1941-50. Chicago: Univ. of Chicago Press.

TAYLOR, J. (1974) China and Southeast Asia: Peking's Relations with Revolutionary Movements. New York: Praeger.

TENG Hsiao-p'ing (1974) Speech at the U.N. General Assembly; text released by New China News Agency (April 10).

TOPPING, S. (1972) Journey Between Two Chinas. New York: Harper & Row.

96

TUCHMAN, B. W. (1972) "If Mao had come to Washington: an essay in alternatives." Foreign Affairs 51, 1 (October): 44-64.

––– (1971) Stilwell and the American Experience in China, 1911-1945. New York: Macmillan.

U.S. Department of State (1975) Conference on Security and Co-Operation in Europe, Final Act, Helsinki. Washington: U.S. Dept. of State.

––– (1966) U.S. Policy with Respect to Mainland China. Washington: U.S. Gov. Printing Office.

U.S. Government (1973) Foreign Relations of the United States, 1948, Vol. VII, The Far East: China. Washington: U.S. Gov. Printing Office.

––– (1972) Testimony of Allen S. Whiting before the Senate Foreign Relations Committee in United States Relations with the People's Republic of China. Washington: U.S. Gov. Printing Office.

––– (1969) Foreign Relations of the United States, 1945, Vol. VII, The Far East: China. Washington: U.S. Gov. Printing Office.

Washington Post (1976a) April 12.
––– (1976b) January 12.
––– (1975a) December 31.
––– (1975b) December 5.
––– (1975c) December 2.
––– (1975d) September 9.
––– (1975e) March 28.
––– (1974) January 16.
––– (1973a) November 18.
––– (1973b) November 14.
––– (1973c) February 19.
––– (1973d) January 29.
––– (1972a) December 29.
––– (1972b) October 27.
––– (1972c) July 3.
––– (1972d) May 24.
––– (1972e) April 20.
––– (1972f) March 18.
––– (1970) July 10.

Washington Star (1976) March 18.
––– (1975a) December 5.
––– (1975b) December 3.

Washington Star-News (1973) November 15.

WHITING, A. S. (1975) The Chinese Calculus of Deterrence: India and Indochina. Univ. of Michigan Press.

––– (1960) China Crosses the Yalu: The Decision to Enter the Korean War. New York: Macmillan.

WILLIAMS, B. (1975) "The Chinese petroleum industry: growth and prospects." pp. 225-263 in China: A Reassessment of the Economy. Washington: U.S. Gov. Printing Office.

YOUNG, K. T. (1968) Negotiating with the Chinese Communists: The United States Experience, 1955-1967. New York: McGraw-Hill.

YUAN-li Wu (1969) As Peking Sees Us. Stanford: Hoover Institution.

ZAGORIA, D. (1962) The Sino-Soviet Conflict, 1956-1961. Princeton, N.J.: Princeton Univ. Press.

ZORZA, V. (1976) Columns in the Washington Post (March 12, 26).